Part One

BOLTON TOWN CENTRE PUBS 1900-2000

The Painters Arms in 1978. The building became the Academy in 1994

Absolutely Fabulous

Clarence Street

In 1986 the former St George's School for Boys, a listed building, opened as the Benjamin Topp public house selling Tetley-Walker beers, with a restaurant on the top floor. In 1990 it was reopened by Honeycomb Restaurants, with a new dance floor and stage. A few years later the name was changed to McGinlay's after its new owner, the former Bolton Wanderers striker. In October 1995 the building was transformed into Absolutely Fabulous fun pub and show bar, and this closed in 1998. In January 2000 the building became a furniture store.

Academy

148-150 Crook Street

Originally the Painters Arms and many years ago a Magees house before being acquired by Hamers of Bromley Cross. Duttons took over Hamers in 1951 and were themselves taken over by Whitbread thirteen years later. The Painters became Scandals in 1984, Mr D's in 1988 and in 1994 the Academy Bar. The premises were boarded up and for sale at the end of 1999.

Albion Hotel

36 Moor Lane

The Albion was originally a beerhouse and was first licensed over a hundred and fifty years ago. For a time it belonged to Leach's Albert Brewery on Derby Street, then to Messrs Cunningham, brewers of Warrington. In 1951 the Albion was one of thirty-four pubs sold to Joshua Tetley & Son of Leeds. It became fully licensed in 1961.

Alma Inn

152 Bradshawgate

The Alma, a former beerhouse, was a Greenall Whitley (formerly Magees) pub until the 1970s. It was closed for over twelve months in 1979-80 whilst repairs and renovations were made, and reopened in 1980 as a Burtonwood pub. Three years later it was doubled in size when it was extended into the former shop next door. There was another major refurbishment in 1992, when the Alma came under the Vantage Inns division of Burtonwood.

The Anchor in 1978

Anchor Inn

14-16 Union Buildings, Bradshawgate

Towards the end of the nineteenth century the Anchor was a beerhouse belonging to Atkinson's Commission Street Brewery. It was later taken over by the Cornbrook brewery and in 1961, the year it became fully licensed, the property passed to Charrington United Breweries, the forerunner of Bass Charrington.

In years gone by the Anchor, together with its former neighbour across the street, the Wellington, and the Brown Cow, the Queens Hotel, the Clarence Hotel and the Alma Inn provided refreshment for the inhabitants of the now-demolished property in Byng Street East, Cunliffe Street and Bradshaw Street, as well as for Breightmet Street residents and workers on the Breightmet Street, River Street, Shiffnall Street, Bradshawgate 'industrial estate'.

Ancient Shepherd

11 Bold Street

The Ancient Shepherd was a beerhouse and in the mid-nineteenth century it was called the Oddfellows Arms. It became fully licensed in 1960.

A typical town centre pub, it was owned by Magees until Greenalls acquired the brewery in the late 1950s. Greenalls sold the property to Thwaites Brewery in the early 1980s. The pub closed in the 1990s.

Angel Inn *See Victoria Buffet*

Balmoral Hotel

94 Bradshawgate
The Balmoral Hotel opened in 1876 and received its licence from an old Deansgate alehouse called the Three Crowns, which was pulled down for Corporation improvements. Following the construction of the Balmoral and Crompton House (now occupied by the Revolution bar) on the other corner of Great Moor Street, the street became much wider at its eastern extremity and took on its present-day look. The Balmoral was a Magees pub before the present owners, Greenalls, took over.

The Bank of England

The Alma in 1978. Five years after this picture was taken the pub was doubled in size when it was extended into the shop premises next door

The Ancient Shepherd in 1978

Bank of England

36 Kay Street
You could stand with your back to this Magees hostelry and announce, 'Well, at least I'll never be broke. I've got the Bank of England behind me'. It was a beerhouse which closed in 1956 and was demolished two years later for the widening of this section of Kay Street.

Bark Street Hotel

251-253 Bark Street
This Magees, later Greenalls, beerhouse stood on the corner of Pool Street and closed in 1969. The site is now part of Pool Street South car park, opened in 1971.

Barley Mow

140 Crook Street
The triangle of land at the corner of Crook Street and Thynne Street, across from Holy Trinity Church, was once used as a bus station. Earlier, there were shops and houses here, together with the Barley Mow on the Burns Street corner, which was licensed to sell beer and wine. In the 1890s the licensee was also a brewer, but Wilsons Brewery was supplying the beer by the time the house closed in 1910.

Bar Peru *See One Horse Shoe*

Bathe's Vaults *See Joiners Arms*

Baths Tavern

42 Bridgeman Place
This beerhouse was closed and demolished in 1927. It stood almost opposite the entrance to Salop Street and was one of seven properties pulled down to make way for an extension to the Globe Works.

Bay Horse

37 Deansgate
George Munro & Co's Bay Horse, popularly known as the 'Scotch

Vaults', was sited on the south side of Deansgate facing Bridge Street, at one of the busiest road junctions in the town centre. It was one of Bolton's oldest licensed houses, dating back to the 1770s or earlier. The building was acquired by Marks & Spencer in June 1959, the licence was surrendered in April 1960 and the property was demolished to make way for Marks & Spencer's store.

Bears Paw *See Brass Cat*

Bee Hive

118 Deansgate
The Bee Hive was one of several properties required for the widening of Deansgate and the licence lapsed in 1900. About 1870 the beerhouse appears to have been jointly owned by the licensees of the nearby Kings Arms and Welcome Home. Later, brewer J G Swales of Hulme, Manchester, was supplying the Bee Hive. The Head Post Office was erected over the site in 1913-16 and opened in November of the latter year.

Bee Hive

1-3 Duke Street
This stood on the corner of Bark Street. A beerhouse, it sold Magees ales a century ago and then was in private hands until Walkers of Warrington acquired the property. The licence was surrendered in 1957, along with that of the Mortfield Tavern on Gaskell Street, in an agreement concerning the transfer of the licence of the Pineapple on Radcliffe Road, Darcy Lever, to the new Castle Hotel on Crompton Way. The site of the Bee Hive is now occupied by Pinewood Studios.

Bay Horse

Benjamin Topp
See Absolutely Fabulous

Bentley's
See Revolution

Bergerac's Wine Bar

St Andrews Court, Mawdsley Street
Bergerac's opened in October 1985 as a satellite of Clouseau's Club, which was at 2 & 4 Mawdsley Street. Like the latter, it took its name from a fictional detective. The basement bar was previously Mr Bojangles' Restaurant, then Massey's and Peter's Cellars.

Big Tub *See Joiners Arms*

Black Bull *See Bull & Wharf*

Black Horse Hotel

15 Blackhorse Street
The Black Horse was the first Bolton residence of Isaac Dobson and was the headquarters of the Black Horse Club, comprising mainly local industrialists and founded by Isaac and Benjamin Dobson, Peter Rothwell and Benjamin Hick. This club was instrumental in securing for Samuel Crompton in his later years an annuity of £63.15s and the great inventor himself frequently attended meetings, 'drinking his one glass of ale, seldom speaking, except when directly addressed and then always briefly and to the point'.

The Black Horse first appears in licensing records in 1801 and in the twentieth century it was a Tongs house (later Walkers). It closed in 1937. The site today is taken up by a widened Blackhorse Street and the green sward of Cheadle Gardens.

Blood Tub *See Red Cross Hotel*

Blue Boar

96 Deansgate
The Blue Boar is one of Bolton's old public houses, dating from the eighteenth century. Among the breweries which have had an interest in the pub over the past hundred years are Magees, Tongs, Hamers (Bromley Cross) and Duttons of Blackburn. It became a Whitbread pub when that company took over the Duttons houses

The Bee Hive on the corner of Duke Street and Bark Street. It became a Walkers house, but in the 1920s it was a free house, as the sign clearly states

in 1964. The Blue Boar was closed for six weeks in 1982 whilst the interior was refurbished and in the 1990s it was styled a Whitbread 'Hogshead' and later a 'Beer Emporium' pub.

Boars Head

39 Churchgate

The Boars Head was built in 1721 and in its early days was one of the town's principal inns. It was also a posting house, a meeting place for the licensing justices, and over the years the venue for many a club and society. The pub was refurbished in 1982, then in 1989 the owners, Greenall Whitley, applied to demolish it along with adjoining buildings. The Boars Head closed in March 1992 and demolition began in January 1998. An archaeological dig on the site revealed a Tudor mullioned window and some late mediaeval walls under the adjoining chip shop and also a well and some mediaeval pottery. In 1999 Wolverhampton & Dudley Breweries built their Varsity bar on the site.

The Boars Head, together with the Farm Produce Shop and Copple's carpet shop in 1966

Bowling Green Tavern

See Brunswick Hotel

Bow Street Tavern

52 Bow Street

This Magees beerhouse stood at the corner of Anvil Street, a short thoroughfare connecting the Crown Street/Bow Street junction with Manor Street. It closed in 1920 and the site of the tavern is now part of Crown Street car park.

Bradford Arms

23 Bridgeman Place

Sharman's (later Shaw's) Bradford Arms closed in 1936. The beerhouse faced the side of the Globe Works and today, a bus lay-by, footpath and part of a car park occupy the site.

The Bradford Arms, Bridgeman Place

The Blue Boar in the 1970s

Brass Cat

13 Churchgate

During the second half of the eighteenth century the Golden Ball Inn stood behind what became Gaskell House, off Churchgate. The licence was subsequently transferred to a building on Churchgate which from about 1772 to 1778 was known as the Bears Paw, from 1779 to 1806 as the Crown & Thistle and from 1806 as the Golden Lion (colloquially 't'Brass Cat'). The property was part of the Earl of Bradford's estate until it was sold to Sharmans Brewery, then in the 1920s it became a Shaws of Leigh house. Walkers of Warrington took over in 1931 and the Golden Lion was a Tetley-Walker house when it became part of the Berni Inn group in the mid-1960s. Until 1962 Booth's music shop occupied part of the building and when Booth's moved to their present shop the pub was doubled in size.

After considerable alterations and extensions it opened as the Golden Lion Steakhouse and public house in 1966. The name Bears Paw was revived in December 1986, when Chef & Brewer reopened the pub and restaurant after alterations. There was another change of name - to the Brass Cat - in 1995, when the business was taken over by the Magic Pub Company. The King Pub Company of London are now the owners.

Brasshouse Bar

14-18 Churchgate
New licensed premises opened on the site of the former Lennon's Supermarket in 1996. The bar is owned by Allied Domecq Leisure.

Brewers Arms

79 Newport Street
The Brewers Arms beerhouse was on the corner of Back Newport Street and once sold the ales of Halliwell's Alexandra Brewery, Mount Street. It closed in 1908 and the site is now covered by Kwik Save supermarket.

Bridge Foot Inn

2-4 St Helena Road
The Bridge Foot was a Sharmans beerhouse which closed in 1934. The building, on the corner of Chorley Street, could still be seen until the 1980s.

The Bridge Foot Inn in the 1920s

(Old) Bridge Inn

31 Bridge Street
The Bridge Inn was located between Rushton Street and Bridge Street and next-door-but-one to the old Fish Market. It was originally called the Gartside Arms and was in existence by 1800. The licence was refused in 1926 and the building was demolished along with the Fish Market for the widening of Bridge Street in the early 1930s.

Britannia Hotel

2-4 Derby Street
For some considerable time the Britannia, an old hostelry dating back to at least 1800, was the headquarters of Bolton Wanderers Football Club. It was a Cornbrook Brewery hostelry, closed in 1965 and demolished as part of a town centre improvement scheme. The site is now green sward alongside Bolton Institute's Deane Campus.

Britannia Hotel

British Oak

37 Union Street
This Sharmans beerhouse was on the corner of Lark Street and closed in 1905. The site is now a landscaped area next to St Peter's Way.

British Queen

144 Newport Street
Atkinson's Commission Street Brewery owned the British Queen beerhouse in the nineteenth century. It was subsequently owned by Cornbrook Brewery, then Magees, and finally Greenall Whitley. The building stood in a prominent position at the south west corner of Newport Street and closed in 1972. It was demolished the following year to make way for an extended Trinity Street.

Brown Cow

153 Bradshawgate
The Brown Cow was a Hamers beerhouse on the corner of Shiffnall Street. It became a Duttons (Blackburn) house in 1951 and was fully licensed in 1961. The Brown Cow and the Queens Hotel next door were both demolished in 1965 and the Trotters was built on the site.

Brunswick Hotel

91 Crook Street
The Brunswick, at the corner of Crook Street and Ormrod Street, was previously the Railway Shipping Inn and even earlier the Bowling Green

Tavern. Originally a beerhouse, the Brunswick became fully licensed when the Old Hen & Chickens on Deansgate closed and the licence was transferred here in 1888. The pub was owned by Atkinson's Commission Street Brewery and from 1898 the Cornbrook Brewery. It closed in 1955 and the full licence was again transferred, this time to the Bulls Head on Bury Road. The Brunswick was eventually demolished about 1968.

'There's a railroad runs through the middle of the house' goes the first line of a well-known old song. Substitute 'street' for 'house', and the words could have been applied to the Brunswick. For most of its years a busy little branch railway line ran across Crook Street and along the centre of Ormrod Street to the huge steel works alongside Moor Lane and the Deansgate goods warehouse.

The British Queen

Bull & Wharf Hotel

12 Church Wharf
The Bull & Wharf Inn, originally the Black Bull, was well situated to serve what became a busy 'port' after the construction of the Manchester, Bolton & Bury Canal at the end of the eighteenth century. Barges transported goods between the three major centres and there was a regular packet boat service for passengers. Many were the bargees and passengers who slaked their thirsts within the Bull & Wharf whilst waiting to start or after completing their three-hour journey to or from Manchester.

The barge trade ceased just after the beginning of the twentieth century but the Bull & Wharf Hotel continued to serve the community which had grown up around it. Finally, in the 1960s the culverting of the River Croal and the need for a new major road, St Peter's Way, brought about the demolition of all the property in the Church Wharf area. The hotel, for a considerable number of years a Sharmans house, passed to Shaws of Leigh and finally to Tetley-Walker. It closed in 1964 and was demolished in 1966.

The Bush Hotel (right), with the Theatre Royal next door and beyond that the Derby Arms. The next building is the Legs of Man

Bulls Head *See Yates's Wine Lodge*

Bush Hotel

14 Churchgate
Originally the Star Inn, opened about 1840. It became the Bush Hotel about 1900. In 1960 Churchgate was the pub and theatreland of Bolton, with seven public houses along its length. The Bush Hotel then belonged to the Cornbrook Brewery, and in the nineteenth century had been the property of Atkinson's Commission Street Brewery. It closed in 1963, the same year as the nearby Derby Arms, and the Brasshouse Bar now covers the site. Along with other past and present hostelries in Churchgate, the Bush Hotel is commemorated in an interesting rhyme of many years ago:

The 'Man and Scythe' that never mowed,
And 'Legs of Man' which never strode,
Also 'Angel and Trumpet' who never blowed,
The 'Golden Lion' that never roared,
A 'Bush' that never growed,

And 'Boars Head' that never snored,
'Rising Sun' and 'Swan' that never soared.
With odd 'Legs and Arms' the gate is stored.

Carrington's

See Revolution

Central Hotel

1-3 Chancery Lane

This was originally the Queen Anne and dated from the eighteenth century. The name was changed to the Central Hotel in the 1890s, when the pub belonged to the Silverwell Brewery. The Manchester Brewery Company took over in 1899 and the licence was refused at the February Sessions in 1911, when the premises were described as being 'ill-conducted' and the licence holder 'unsatisfactory'. The building was later used for various purposes and from 1946 housed departments of Tillotson's Newspapers Ltd. The site at the corner of Ship Gates is now covered by the C&A Store which opened in November 1970.

The Bull & Wharf in the 1920s

Cheers

Nelson House, Bradshawgate

The short-lived Cheers bar occupied part of the prominent building on the corner of Nelson Square which was formerly Prudential House and is now part of Red on the Square. Cheers opened in 1994, then in 1996 the licence was transferred to Durty Nelly's.

The Church Hotel in the 1920s

Chester Moonshines

See Revolution

Chicago Rock Cafe

Bridge Street

Part of the new development on the site of the old Bridge Street Co-op buildings, this bar opened in September 1998.

Chorley Tavern

See Manchester House

Church Hotel

174 Crook Street

The Church Hotel opened within a few years of the consecration of Holy Trinity Church and now survives it. The hotel was one of twenty-one Tongs Brewery houses acquired by Walkers of Warrington in 1923 and later became a Tetley pub. Today it remains a popular establishment with a substantial gay clientele.

Clarence Hotel

176 Bradshawgate

The Clarence was built by Rowland Hall Heaton, a local joiner, builder and timber merchant, who in 1836 had built a cotton factory in Dawes Street. Mr Heaton obtained his public house licence in 1844, but he died the following year. The Clarence remained in his family for some time afterwards. It was in the hands of the Manchester Brewery Company of Ardwick at the end of the nineteenth century and was acquired by Magees in 1941. The Clarence was a Greenalls pub when it was pulled down in the early 1990s along with other property fronting Bradshawgate, and JJB Sports now covers the site.

Clifton Arms

94 Newport Street

In the 1870s this was a beerhouse called the Newport Hotel. The name was changed to the Clifton and for a time it was one of the tied houses of James Leach, Albert Brewery, Derby Street. It was later acquired by the Empress Brewery of Manchester and then passed to Walkers of Warrington in 1929. The pub became fully licensed in 1962 and the building was given a major facelift and extension by Tetley-Walker in 1986.

The Clifton Arms

Club Liquid *See Space City*

Club Uropa *See Pink Panther*

Coach & Horses

123-125 Deansgate

The Coach & Horses was a late eighteenth century hostelry which stood on the corner of Back Spring Gardens and closed in 1907, when it was owned by the Manchester Brewery Company. The YMCA and shop property cover the site.

Cock & Trumpet
See Levers Arms Hotel

Commercial Hotel

2 Victoria Square

From its commanding position on the north side of Bolton's town centre precinct, this hotel saw many town centre changes, particularly in the area immediately in front of it. The Commercial Tavern opened in 1809 in an area which became known as the New Market Place and the hostelry served its stallholders and customers. Bolton Town Hall opened in 1873 and over the succeeding years looked down on its near neighbour, which in its turn watched benevolently for many years over a regular succession of travelling fairs and menageries. Always a popular meeting and eating establishment, the Commercial also had a long association with politics and in the nineteenth century was frequently used as a political headquarters. The Town Hall Square subsequently replaced the New Market Square, became Victoria Square in 1897 and the present precinct in 1969.

The Commercial was run for many years until the 1870s by the Brandwood family and it subsequently became a Magees house. Greenall Whitley were the owners in April 1972 when, despite many protests, the hotel closed. The building was demolished the following November and on the site arose the present Mothercare store, opened in August 1974.

Chancery Lane and the former Central Hotel

Concert Tavern

28 Churchgate

The Concert Tavern was a beerhouse, owned by Atkinson's Commission Street Brewery in the 1890s and then by Bolton Theatre & Entertainment Company Ltd. It closed in 1908, when Tongs Brewery appear to have been the lessees, for extensions to the Grand Theatre. The Grand was demolished in 1963 and the site is now occupied by part of Churchgate House.

Corks Wine Bar *See O'Neill's*

Cottons

Bradshawgate

This opened as one of Whitbread's Hogshead real ale bars in 1995, in the building on the corner of Silverwell Street which had once served as a post office and then as an employment exchange. In early 1998 the pub became Hogs, then Cottons.

Cotton Tree Inn

9 Edgar Street

The Cotton Tree was a beerhouse, owned by the Mort family when it closed in 1908. It was leased to the Silverwell Brewery and latterly to the Manchester Brewery Company. The site is now part of the curve of the extended Trinity Street.

Crate Egg *See Market Hotel*

Crompton's Mule

Bradshawgate

Crompton's Mule was formerly the Prince William and one of Bolton's oldest pubs. In the eighteenth century the hostelry on this site was called the Hope & Anchor. It became the Prince William of Gloucester (to give the full title) about 1803 and in the 1830s and 1840s it was one of Bolton's coaching inns. Magees, the Silverwell Brewery and the Manchester Brewery Company all had an interest in the property at one time or another. The pub was rebuilt in 1921 by J G Swales & Co of Manchester and this brewery's name could still be seen on the building in the 1990s, although the brewery itself was taken over by Boddingtons in 1971.

In the early 1970s a balustrade and cupola were removed from the top of the building and in 1983 the pub was closed for five months for extensive alterations to the interior. The Prince William was re-styled Sam's Bar in 1990 and then in July 1996 reopened as Crompton's Mule. Later alterations included extending the pub, now owned by Greenalls Inns, across the site of the former shop next door.

The Hogshead on Bradshawgate. It became Cottons in 1998

Crompton's Mule

Spa Road - see Hawthorns

Cromwellian Club *See Villiers Hotel*

Cross Street Tavern *See Griffin Inn*

Crown & Cushion

8 Mealhouse Lane

A 1781 sale notice declared that at numbers 6 and 7 in a certain street called the Acres or Mealhouse Lane, two dwelling houses were 'now occupied and used as a public house known by the sign of the Crown and Cushion...' This old Crown & Cushion was demolished in 1900 for the building of the imposing Empress Hall, which incorporated a new Crown & Cushion. For many years until his death in 1929 Bolton-born Albert Shepherd, Bolton Wanderers and England footballer, was licensee of the hostelry.

Tong's (later Walker's) Crown & Cushion closed in March 1971 and, along with adjoining brewery offices and an off licence, was converted into shop premises, first Tracks and later the National & Provincial Building Society. The Empress Hall served the public faithfully as a dance hall for over sixty-five years before it became the Club Empress and, from 1978, Spencer's Club and Bar, named after and owned by three times World Snooker Champion John Spencer. In 1988 it was announced that the Crown & Cushion was returning, but fifteen feet higher than it used to be. The new pub opened in August in the old ballroom. In 1990 the Bolton Evening News announced that 'Karaoke fever was gripping the town' and the Crown & Cushion installed a hi-tech machine so that 'Even a mediocre singer can sound something like a rock star.' Today the Crown & Cushion is styled a 'Pub-Club' and includes the Mealhouse Restaurant and the Centre Cue snooker and pool club.

The Crown & Cushion

Crown & Thistle

See Brass Cat

Derby Arms

22 Churchgate

At the end of the nineteenth century the Derby Arms belonged to Atkinson's Commission Street Brewery. It became a Cornbrook pub in 1898 and was still selling Cornbrook beers when it closed in 1963. Churchgate House was built on the site. (See Bush Hotel)

Derby Hotel

2-4 Chorley Street

This beerhouse occupied a corner of Chorley Street and St Helena Road and for many years faced the Bridge Foot Inn. The Derby Hotel closed in 1921 and the site is now covered by part of a works yard.

Dirty Habits

2-4 Manor Street

A 'Fun Pub' which opened for a short period in 1999.

Dog & Partridge

Manor Street

The Dog & Partridge, which dates from the beginning of the nineteenth century, was a Cornbrook house for many years before being acquired by Bass. There was another change of brewery in 1978, when the present owners, Thwaites, took over.

Dog & Partridge

90 Moor Lane

The Dog & Partridge opened in the late eighteenth century and was one of a handful of hostelries which, in the nineteenth century, housed a private theatre. For some years it was a Tongs house and then by the time it closed in 1969 it belonged to Tetley-Walker. Bolton Corporation served a compulsory purchase order on the pub, which stood at the corner of Partridge Street, along with the Lancashire Dairy Ration Company's factory and Howarth's potato warehouse. The construction of Bolton's new Fire Station began later that year and this was opened in February 1971. The site of the Dog & Partridge now fronts the fire station buildings.

The Railway on Great Moor Street, later Donaghy's.

Donaghy's

63 Great Moor Street

At one time this was a beerhouse called the Ormrod Arms and until the 1980s it was the Railway Inn. It was a Magees house and then for many years belonged to Sharmans Brewery; a distinctive Sharmans sign could still be seen until 1985. That year Tetley sold the Railway to Regal Knight Hotels of Wood Street, Bolton. The pub closed in the May and after extensive alterations reopened as a free house called the Quill and Pen in December. In the 1990s there was another change of ownership and the pub became Donaghy's. In December 1999, after being closed for some time, the building was demolished.

Druids Arms

5 Back Spring Gardens

The Druids was a beerhouse which belonged to the Commission Street Brewery and then Cornbrook Brewery. It closed in 1910 and the site is now part of the Police Station on Howell Croft North.

Duck & Firkin *See Trotters Hotel*

Duke of Cambridge Hotel

97 Bark Street

A Magees, later Greenalls, house which stood on the left-hand side of Bark Street from Knowsley Street and just over half way between the latter and Duke Street. The pub closed in 1967 for redevelopment and today a new building containing a branch of Gregory and Porritt's stands on the site.

Duke of Clarence Hotel

39 Bath Street

The Duke of Clarence was originally a beerhouse and became fully licensed when the Horse & Groom, Bradshawgate, closed in 1875 and the

The Dog & Partridge, Moor Lane, in the 1920s

spirit licence was transferred here. It became a Threlfalls house, then Whitbread when the London-based brewery acquired Threlfall-Chesters in 1967. The pub was demolished in 1996 after being closed for some time. The site is now a car park.

Durty Nelly's

Bradshawgate

This Irish theme pub, owned by the St James Group of Newcastle, opened in May 1996 in what had been Cheadle's confectioner's shop. The licence came from the Cheers bar on the corner of Nelson Square.

Eagle & Child

Manchester Court, Spring Gardens

The Eagle & Child was an old public house, first licensed in the late eighteenth century and a Tongs house when it closed in 1906. The site is now covered by part of the rear of Le Mans Crescent.

Eagle & Vulcan

45 Folds Road

Originally a beerhouse, this Magees (later Greenall Whitley) pub stood on the corner of Hulme Street. It closed in 1968 for the construction of a dual carriageway along Folds Road. The site is now covered by the road and part of the bridge which carries St Peter's Way over it.

Elephant & Castle

14 Blackhorse Street

The Elephant & Castle was first licensed in 1804 and stood opposite the Black Horse Hotel. When it closed in 1904 the licence was one of three surrendered by Magees in return for a full licence for the Pike View beerhouse on Derby Street. The site of the Elephant & Castle is now part of the area in front of the Crown Court building.

The Duke of Clarence in the 1950s

Durty Nelly's

Back Spring Gardens and the Druids Arms in 1908

Empire Lounge

46 Bradshawgate

The Empire Lounge, with its Axminster carpets and mahogany fittings, was a splendid replacement for the Volunteer Inn, according to the Bolton Evening News in 1890. The Volunteer had stood here for around a hundred years and the earliest records show it was originally called the Jolly Sailor. The Empire Lounge lasted only fifteen years: the licence was refused in 1904 and the building was pulled down for the widening of Bradshawgate. At one time or another four brewing companies had interests in the property - Tongs, Atkinsons, Allsopp of Burton-on-Trent and Magees. The frontage of Crompton Place now covers the site.

Flag Hotel

62 Great Moor Street

Licensed houses with the name 'Flag Hotel' are usually so called because the inn sign takes the form of a Union Jack, but there is a rather different story told about Bolton's Flag Hotel. It is said that over 150 years ago eight dray horses with chains and rollers were used to transport a huge flagstone, fifteen feet square and weighing six tons, from a local quarry to this house on the corner of Great Moor Street and Howell Croft. The stone was used to cover part of the floor of the building.

The Flag first appears in the records in 1825 and in later years it was a Magees house, then passed into the control of Greenall Whitley. It was closed in November 1970 and demolished three months later. The site is now part of a car park.

Flax Tavern *See Queens Arms*

Fleece Inn *See Maxim's*

Eagle & Child

Flag Hotel

Flying Horse

38-40 Crook Street

This beerhouse stood on the corner of Crook Street and Great Moor Street and was owned by the Empress Brewery of Old Trafford, Manchester, when it closed in 1924. The site is covered by the curve of the extended Trinity Street.

Founders Arms

30-32 Ashburner Street

First licensed in 1806 as the Founders Inn, this Magees house on the corner of Howell Croft South closed in 1926. In the July the public house licence was transferred to the newly-opened Brooklyn Hotel on Green Lane. The site was later acquired for building the Civic Centre and is now occupied by part of the Libraries Department.

Founders Arms

18 St George's Street

Hope Iron Foundry once stood on the corner of St George's Street and All Saints Street, a site later occupied by Moscrop's oil works. The Founders Arms opened on the opposite corner in the 1830s. It became a Sharmans house, then Walkers and Tetleys and today belongs to Burtonwood Brewery.

The Founders Arms in the 1920s

Four Horse Shoes
See Silver Vat

Gaiety *See Maxim's*

Gartside Arms
See (Old) Bridge Inn

George & Dragon

13-15 Oxford Street

The George & Dragon dated from the eighteenth century and stood on the west side of Oxford Street. It was a Sharmans house when it closed in 1924 and was demolished to make way for the huge Co-operative Society store, opened in 1928 and closed in 1986.

George Hotel

92 Great Moor Street

Just as the former Railway Hotel on the corner of Trinity Street and Newport Street served travellers from the nearby railway station, so the George was popular with those using Great Moor Street Station. In fact, in the nineteenth century this hostelry, which was diagonally across the road from the former station, was for a time called the George Inn and Railway Hotel. The pub dates from around 1820 and was owned by the Manchester Brewery Company in the 1880s. It became a Walker & Homfray house and then a Wilsons house in 1949. In more recent times it was acquired by John Smiths.

Gipsy's Tent

178 Deansgate

This former Sharmans beerhouse was cut off from the rest of Deansgate in 1877 when Marsden Road was constructed. It became fully licensed in 1961, when it was a Tetley-Walker house. The Gipsy's Tent closed late in 1983 and after extensive alterations reopened as Winstons in September 1984. After a few years it became the Gipsy's Tent again, with Romany's function room upstairs.

Globe Vaults *See Market Hotel*

Golden Ball *See Brass Cat*

Golden Cup

129 Newport Street

The Golden Cup was a beerhouse belonging to Halliwell's Alexandra Brewery and after it closed in 1905 the building became a shop. It was practically opposite the entrance to Taylor Street and was demolished in 1986 to make way for the bus/rail interchange.

Golden Lion *See Brass Cat*

Oxford Street and the George & Dragon in 1907

The George in 1961

The Grapes, Victoria Square, in the 1920s

Goose with Two Necks
See Market Hotel

Grapes Hotel

33 Victoria Square

The Grapes was a typical basic town centre pub with entrances on Victoria Square and in Exchange Street. It was a Sharmans house, then Walkers, and when it was closed and demolished in 1960 the building was 120 years old. All that block of property facing the Town Hall was pulled down and new shops built. Today, the shops between Exchange Street and Back Cheapside occupy the site of the Grapes Hotel.

Grapes Hotel

20 Water Street

In July 1818 a quintet of Bolton businessmen became partners in an historic banking venture, using wine merchant Robert Barlow's premises in Water Street. After many years the business moved to the corner of Market Street and Corporation Street, and in 1875 to what is now the Royal Bank of Scotland building on the corner of Deansgate and Market Street. The building in Water Street became a beerhouse called the Grapes Hotel and ended its days in September 1952 as a Magees hostelry. Today the site of the Grapes is a nothingness, a patch of sloping ground on which trees grow and which weeds have colonised. Most of Water Street is now obliterated by the Folds Road car park.

Greyhound

147 Deansgate

The Greyhound was a beerhouse, first licensed in the mid-nineteenth century, and before that the premises were a baker's shop. It was owned by Atkinson's Commission Street Brewery and then the Cornbrook Brewery before becoming a Bass Charrington house in 1961. A full licence was acquired in April 1961, at the same time as the nearby Gipsy's Tent. The Greyhound is sometimes referred to as 't'Kickin' Donkey', a nickname which may simply derive from a badly painted greyhound on the signboard. However, the story goes that a customer of many years ago used to tether his donkey outside whilst he imbibed, and this animal would kick out at any unsuspecting passer-by who happened to walk too close to it!

Grey Man

138 Great Moor Street

The Grey Man was the last building on the right of Great Moor Street before Derby Street. It was a Magees beerhouse (later Greenall Whitley) and became fully licensed in 1962. The Grey Man ceased trading in 1972 and the building was demolished for the widening of Derby Street as part of the Trinity Street extension.

The Griffin in 1978. Great Moor Street boasted ten hostelries in the 1930s: Balmoral, New Zealand Chief, Flag, Railway, George, Grey Man, Peacock, Griffin, Vulcan and Wheatsheaf. Today only the Balmoral, Griffin and George remain

Grey Mare

6 Newport Street

In his 'Historical Gleanings of Bolton and District', local historian Barton notes that the premises which housed the Grey Mare public house were built expressly for the publication of the old Bolton Chronicle, which began in 1824. The building, on the corner of Back Exchange Street, continued in this use until the 1830s. It was subsequently licensed as a beerhouse and became the Grey Mare public house in 1844. It was later a Tongs, then a Walkers hostelry and closed in 1957. The licence was transferred to the new Mosley Arms, Red Lane.

Griffin Inn

45 Great Moor Street

In a twenty-year period during the late nineteenth and early twentieth centuries this former beerhouse had three names - the Soho Street Tavern, the Cross Street Tavern and the Griffin Inn. It was a tied house of Atkinson's Commission Street Brewery and then the Cornbrook Brewery from 1898. Bass became the owners in the 1960s and in the 1990s the Griffin was acquired by Mercury Taverns.

Hand & Banner

113-115 Deansgate

The Hand & Banner was on the south side of Deansgate, between Spring Gardens and Back Spring Gardens, and like its near neighbour, the Coach & Horses, it opened in the late eighteenth century. The Hand & Banner survived a few years longer and closed in 1911. The site is now covered by the Lloyds TSB Bank building.

Hare & Hounds *See Villiers Hotel*

Harp Tavern

109 Moor Lane

This Magees beerhouse stood between Back Crook Street and Flash Street and closed in 1913. Many years later the premises became the Harp Garage. The site is now part of the road junction between Sainsbury's store and Deane Road.

Harvey's Cafe Bar

Mawdsley Street

This opened in December 1995 as Henry's Cafe Bar with a licence transferred from Magees (formerly the Crofters, see Part Two) on St George's Road. The name was changed to Harvey's in 1999.

Hawthorns

Spa Road

Hawthorns opened as Cromptons Mule bistro bar in December 1978, in

The Grapes Hotel, Water Street

property which once housed a garage and grain store. Several months later a restaurant was added and in 1984, following a sizeable extension, the whole took on the title Hawthorns Piano Bar & Bistro. Today it is styled Hawthorns Live Music Venue.

Hen & Chickens

143 Deansgate

Although its sign simply bears the title Hen & Chickens, the name on the licensing register is Higher Hen & Chickens. The reason for this is that until 1888 there was another Hen & Chickens on the other side of Deansgate, next door-but-one to the Kings Arms (now Sweetens bookshop). The Higher Hen & Chickens was in existence in the eighteenth century and the property was rebuilt in 1907. It was a Magees house until Greenall Whitley took over in 1959. The brewery restyled the pub in 1982 and there was a suggestion that it might be pulled down in 1993, but happily it has survived.

Henry's Cafe Bar *See Harvey's*

Hero's Fun Pub *See Villiers Hotel*

High Society *See Space City*

Higher Hen & Chickens
See Hen & Chickens

The Howcroft is one of six Bolton hostelries which appear in CAMRA's Good Beer Guide 2000. The photograph was taken in the 1920s

Higher Nags Head

63 Deansgate

The Higher Nags Head was built in 1735 as a town residence and was converted into a public house some years afterwards. It was known as Holden's Vaults, after the wine and spirit merchant who ran the business for many years. The pub was a Magees house when it closed in 1929. It was demolished a year later and new shops were built on the site, between Market Street and Oxford Street.

The Higher Nags Head in the 1920s

Hogshead *See Cottons*

Holden's Vaults
See Higher Nags Head

Hole i'th'Wall

20 Ashburner Street

A Magees beerhouse which closed in 1931. It stood on the north side of Ashburner Street, between Howell Croft South and Old Hall Street South. The site is now covered by part of the Octagon Theatre.

Hope & Anchor *See Crompton's Mule*

Horse Shoe *See Silver Vat*

Howcroft Inn

Pool Street

Formerly known as the Prince of Wales, the Howcroft was a Sharmans beerhouse before being acquired by Walkers of Warrington. A full licence was granted in 1957. The Howcroft's bowling green was well over a century old when it was closed in November 1980 because the land was on the line of Topp Way. A new green was opened in May 1982. The green was protected by a false floor when a marquee was erected over it in 1994 so that the Howcroft could be the venue for a beer festival, selling around a hundred different real ales. Since then the Bolton Beer Festival has been an annual event at the pub.

Hulme Street Tavern

11-13 Hulme Street

The Hulme Street Tavern stood between the Eagle & Vulcan and the Spread Eagle. It was a Magees beerhouse and closed in 1905. The premises were later used as a grocer's shop and the site is now a grassed area alongside St Peter's Way.

Imperial Hotel

3-5 Church Bank

This was originally known as the Rising Sun and was in existence by the 1770s. It closed in 1934 and the full licence was transferred to the Kings Arms on Chorley Old Road. The building subsequently became a guest house and later, at the end of the 1960s, the home of several small businesses. In its heyday it provided bed and breakfast for artistes who were appearing at the nearby Grand Theatre and Theatre Royal. The building can still be seen.

The Kings Arms in the 1920s

Indian Chief *See New Zealand Chief*

Joiners Arms

15a Deansgate

The Joiners Arms can still be seen on Deansgate, opposite the Old Three Crowns. The main bar room was positioned at the rear of the premises and three shops still front the huge building. Above the shop windows, the ornate façade has changed little since the pub closed more than forty years ago. The building dates from the 1870s, but it replaced a much older Joiners Arms which was in existence in the late eighteenth century. In the 1850s it was run by a wine and spirit merchant called Henry Bathe and known as Bathe's Vaults. In later years it was 't'Big Tub'. Threlfalls Brewery acquired the Joiners Arms in 1891 and they sold it in 1958, when the licence was given up.

Jolly Drummer

16 Partridge Street

The Jolly Drummer was a beerhouse belonging to Tongs Brewery. It closed in 1912 and for many years the building was used as a lodging house. The site is now part of Moor Lane Fire Station.

Jolly Sailor *See Empire Lounge*

Junction Inn

21-23 Howell Croft North

This was a Tongs beerhouse which closed in 1908. The site is fronting and part of the Police Station.

Junction Inn

10 St Helena Road

The Junction Inn beerhouse stood on the south side of St Helena Road, a few doors from the Bridge Foot Inn and in the shadow of the Marsden Road bridge. It closed in 1906.

Jungle Fun Pub *See Pink Panther*

Kicking Donkey *See Greyhound*

Kings Arms

86 Deansgate

The eighteenth century building can still be seen, occupied since 1980 by Sweetens Bookshop. The pub sold the beers of Jackson's Spa Wells Brewery until the 1920s, when Shaws of Leigh took over. It was a later a Walkers house and closed in March 1962. For many years the building remained empty, then from 1974 until 1980 it was the Chapter & Verse religious bookshop.

The Kings Head Hotel in the 1920s

Kings Head Hotel

145-147 Deansgate

The Kings Head was next door to the Hen & Chickens, near the corner of Blackhorse Street. It dated from the end of the eighteenth century and at one time was a Magees pub. Later it became a Tongs house and in its final years was owned by Tetley-Walker. The Kings Head closed in 1968 and, along with a small shop adjoining, was demolished a year later for the widening of Blackhorse Street.

Kiss Night Spot *See Space City*

Legs of Man

24 Churchgate

The Legs of Man was a Groves & Whitnalls house in its final years, although some time before it had been a Tongs Brewery house and earlier still had sold Magees ales. The pub was in existence in the 1790s and closed in March 1962. Churchgate House now covers the site. (See Bush Hotel)

Levers Arms Hotel

13 Nelson Square

This substantial and well-known Magees hotel, often referred to as the 'Cock & Trumpet', opened at the corner of Nelson Square and Bowkers Row about 1830. It was demolished in December 1949 and an extension to the Pack Horse Hotel was erected on its site and opened in August 1952.

Demolition in progress at the Levers Arms Hotel

Lions Paw *See Silver Vat*

Loader's Vaults *See Sun Inn*

Lower Nags Head

47-49 Deansgate

This was called the Lower Nags Head because until 1930 there was a Higher Nags Head on Deansgate, between Market Street and Oxford Street. The original, eighteenth-century Lower Nags Head was pulled down in 1927 for road widening and in December of that year Magees Brewery opened an imposing three-storey hotel. In 1967 it really became the 'Lower' Nags Head when the two bars at ground level were closed and the downstairs lounge was extended into a former cellar area. After considerable alterations Hepworth's tailor's moved into the ground floor in May 1967. There were further alterations to the pub in 1982 and three years later the name was changed to Oliver's. This closed in 1989, and today the only evidence of the pub's existence is the 'MM & Co Ltd' at the top of the building which houses the Abbey National.

The first Lower Nags Head, pulled down in 1927

McGinlay's *See Absolutely Fabulous*

(Old) Man & Scythe

6 Churchgate

The Man & Scythe is the oldest public house in Bolton and tradition suggests that there was an inn on the site in 1251, when Bolton received its market charter. It was rebuilt in 1636 and fifteen years later the Seventh Earl of Derby spent his last few hours there before he was executed in Churchgate. The pub, nicknamed the 'cider house', is owned by Whitbreads Brewery. Earlier, it was a Duttons house and until 1959 belonged to the Bury Crown Brewery. The Man & Scythe closed for a ten-week refit in 1998 and reopened in the April with an altered bar layout and the old courtyard at the back incorporated into the pub.

The Man & Scythe in the 1950s

Manchester House

11 Trinity Street

This beerhouse stood next to the British Queen, Newport Street, and in the nineteenth century belonged to Atkinson's Commission Street Brewery. It was earlier known as the Chorley Tavern (up to about 1883) and became a Cornbrook Brewery house before closing in 1910. The building was subsequently used by the Dexter printing company and the site was eventually swallowed up by the extended Trinity Street.

Market Hotel

10-12 Ashburner Street
Before becoming fully licensed this was a beerhouse, listed as the Goose with Two Necks in 1849 and later as the Globe Vaults. It stood on the corner of Old Hall Street South and the name was changed to the Market Hotel in the 1870s when Bolton's wholesale market was sited across the road. In 1879 the Cross Axes in Woods Court, Deansgate, closed and its full licence was transferred to the Market Hotel. The pub's nickname, 't'Crate Egg', is said to derive from the fact that numerous wooden crates filled with eggs for the market were unloaded nearby.

In the 1890s the Market Hotel belonged to Atkinson's Commission Street Brewery and then the Cornbrook Brewery of Manchester. The licence expired in October 1957 and the building was demolished later that year to make way for the new shops on Newport Street.

Masons Arms

23 King Street
The Masons Arms was a beerhouse and belonged to Atkinsons Commission Street Brewery in the latter part of the nineteenth century. It passed to the Cornbrook Brewery and after the licence was given up in 1906 the building became a lodging house. The site is now covered by a car park.

Matilda's *See Pink Panther*

Old Hall Street South and the Market Hotel in the 1950s

Maxim's

28 Bradshawgate
The eighteenth century Fleece Inn was demolished for road-widening in 1907 and the present building was erected. The original property was part of the Earl of Bradford's estate and the new pub was a Sharmans house before passing to Walkers of Warrington. It was called the Fleece Hotel until 1972, when the name was changed to the Gaiety. In 1980 Tetley-Walker sold the hostelry to Vaux Breweries. Two adjoining shops were incorporated into the licensed premises in 1983 and the whole reopened as Maxim's in July of that year.

Maxwell's Plum *See Villiers Hotel*

Menai Bridge

141 Bradshawgate
This Tongs beerhouse stood near the corner of Shiffnall Street and the licence lapsed in 1901. The building was pulled down to make room for new Transport Offices, which opened in 1906. The site is now occupied by an Ian Anthony car showroom.

Milestone Hotel

5-7 Deane Road
In 1900 the Milestone was owned by Walker's Bolton Brewery of Spa Road, later the Spa Wells Brewery Company and from 1904 the Model Brewery of James Jackson & Sons. Jacksons were taken over by Shaws of Leigh in 1927 and the Milestone eventually became a Walkers house. It was a beerhouse and closed in 1965. The site is now fronting a grassed area alongside Bolton Institute's Deane Campus.

Millstone Hotel

12 Crown Street
The Millstone opened around 1830, a replacement for the Old Millstone which stood on the corner of Deansgate and Pepper Alley (which when widened became Crown Street). Licensee Thomas Sharples established a museum and concert hall at the hotel in 1832 and this was Bolton's earliest music hall. The effect music halls were having on public morals in the 1850s led magistrates to suspend the licence for a time. One wonders what these

Maxims in the days when it was called the Fleece Hotel and part of the building was occupied by two shops

gentlemen would have thought of the topless barmaids who brought the Millstone into the news in 1996!

It was a Sharmans pub in the early twentieth century and latterly belonged to Tetley-Walker. The building was revamped in 1986 and again ten years later after a period of closure. In 1999 Holts Brewery bought the Millstone and in 2000 submitted plans to extend the premises into the old H Rigby & Co building on Bank Street to create a pub/restaurant.

The Millstone Hotel in 1978

Moss Rose

12-14 Charles Street

The Moss Rose was on the right hand side of Charles Street, between Kay Street and Union Street. It was a Tong's beerhouse and closed in 1905. The site is now a landscaped area between a factory/workshop and Union Street.

Mr D's *See Academy*

New Bridge Inn

15 Church Bank

The New Bridge Inn was a beerhouse, earlier known as the Printers Arms, which closed in 1907. For a time it belonged to the Silverwell Brewery and then the Manchester Brewery Company. The licence was surrendered in return for permission to rebuild the Crofters on St George's Road (see Part Two). The New Bridge Inn building was later used as a lodging house and the site is now the vacant land lower down Church Bank from the former Imperial Hotel.

The Milestone in the 1920s

New Market Inn

40 Bridge Street

The New Market Inn was a Magees beerhouse on the corner of Bow Street and when it closed in 1973 it belonged to Greenalls. The building was demolished in 1974 and today the site is a private car park enclosed by advertisement hoardings.

Newport Hotel *See Clifton Arms*

Newport Vaults

104 Newport Street

The Newport Vaults was a Tongs beerhouse which closed in 1924. The building can still be seen, now shop property between the York and the Clifton.

New Zealand Chief

5 Great Moor Street

Until alterations in 1959, this Magees establishment claimed to have the smallest bar in England. It measured only six feet by two feet two inches and a story was often told that a man of more than twenty stones failed to win a bet that he could pull himself a pint from the bar's single set of pumps. He became wedged while attempting to do so. The pub was originally a beerhouse and is named in the 1849 list as the 'Indian Chief'. It became fully licensed in 1961 and survived as a Greenalls house until December 1984. Two years later the building was demolished to make way for the office premises near the corner of Johnson Street.

Oddfellows Arms

93 Bradshawgate

Owned by Seed's (Radcliffe) Brewery and later Magees, the Oddfellows Arms closed in 1938. It subsequently became shop premises and in its last days housed Marie's hairdressing establishment. The building was demolished in 1962 to make way for Metrolands House.

Oddfellows Arms

Bold Street - see Ancient Shepherd

Old Cock Tavern

13 Green Street

A former Tongs beerhouse which closed in 1935. The site is now adjoining and part of the Folds Road car park.

Old Millstone

See Millstone Hotel

The New Market Inn

Old Three Crowns

14 Deansgate

The Old Three Crowns can trace its origins to the eighteenth century and in the latter part of the nineteenth century it was owned by Wingfields Silverwell Brewery. The Manchester Brewery Company took over in 1899, followed by Walker & Homfrays of Salford in 1912 and Wilsons Brewery in 1949. There were considerable alterations to the interior in 1975 and more major alterations and extensions in 1984. The original front entrance was closed and a new entrance was made via the once gated passageway alongside the pub. Today the pub boasts an all-weather, heated beer garden.

The Old Cock in the 1920s

Old Three Tuns Hotel

97 Moor Lane

In this Magees (later Greenalls) hostelry, Bolton Harriers was formed in 1908. The hotel was first licensed in 1804 and it survived until about 1973. The site is now part of the planted area at the side of Sainsbury's store, across from the fire station.

Oliver's

See Lower Nags Head

One Horse Shoe

10 Manor Street

The One Horse Shoe dated from the eighteenth century and it became a coaching house. In the 1820s this was where you boarded the 'Accommodation' coach for Manchester (every morning at 8.00am) and in the 1840s the 'Prince Albert' and the 'Red Rover' coaches departed every Monday afternoon for Haslingden and Ramsbottom respectively. It was later a Magees pub and after closure in 1966 the premises were acquired by Gentleman John Wallpapers. In the 1990s the building became licensed premises once more, the Bar Peru.

O'Neill's

Bradshawgate

The premises were once occupied as a branch of the National Provincial Bank. The bank closed in 1973 and the building was reopened as Corks Wine Bar in July 1979. It became O'Neill's in 1997.

Corks Cafe Bar, which became O'Neill's in 1997

Ormrod Arms *See Donaghy's*

Oscar's Cafe Bar

Wellsprings, Howell Croft South

Opened in 1989.

Pack Horse Hotel

62 Bradshawgate/Nelson Square

In August 1904 a single-storey structure fronting Bradshawgate, all that remained of the eighteenth century Pack Horse Inn, was taken down. The licence continued for nearly eighteen months in a wooden building at the rear until more elaborate premises were opened in 1906. Forty-three years later the old Levers Arms Hotel in Nelson Square was demolished and the Pack Horse was extended over the site. The work took three years. There was another extension in 1962, when Magees acquired and demolished the old Reform Club in Bowkers Row. In December 1983 a new Cotton Bar was opened and in February 1986 Finlay's Restaurant, a tribute to locally-born actor Frank Finlay, was opened in the former Carvery.

In 1995 West Lothian-based Macdonald Hotels acquired the Pack Horse from the De Vere Group, a subsidiary of Greenall Whitley. The Cotton Bar was transformed into O'Leary's Irish Bar, which was opened in February 1996 by Jack Charlton. Finlay's restaurant was moved upstairs and renamed the Oak Room, and the Shawgates Cafe Bar on the Nelson Square side replaced the Regency Lounge.

The Old Three Crowns in the 1950s, showing the original entrance and passageway

Great Moor Street and the Peacock Inn, next door to Smith's fireplace shop

Painters Arms *See Academy*

Parkfield Inn

109 Crook Street

The Parkfield was a Tongs, then Walkers beerhouse which stood on the corner of Dawes Street, about a hundred yards along Crook Street from the Sweet Green Tavern. It closed in 1973 and was demolished to make way for the Trinity Street extension. The last licensee of the Parkfield, Mrs Annie Hamer, had lived on the premises for some fifty years.

Peacock Inn

137 Great Moor Street

The Peacock was a small beerhouse belonging to Groves & Whitnall of Salford and later to Greenalls. It became fully licensed in 1961 and closed in 1973. The property was demolished for the extension of Trinity Street.

Peel Hotel

52 Higher Bridge Street

The Peel Hotel, once a Threlfalls Brewery house, was later owned by Magees and was a Greenalls pub when it closed in April 1985. It stood on the corner of Falcon Street, which was widened to connect Topp Way with St Peter's Way.

Pineapple Inn

25 Water Street

Before 1900 this was the Sweet Home beerhouse. It was owned by Halliwell's Alexandra Brewery until 1910, when Magees took over, and closed in 1934. The site is now part of the Folds Road car park.

Pink Panther

St George's Road

The Pink Panther piano bar and restaurant opened in December 1985. There was an extensive refurbishment in 1990, then in 1994 the premises became Matilda's, an Australian theme bar. A new licence was granted in 1998 to the Jungle Fun Pub, which soon afterwards became Club Uropa.

Playmate *See Villiers Hotel*

Prince of Wales

3 Paley Street

Atkinsons Commission Street Brewery owned this beerhouse, earlier known as the Royal Oak, at the end of the nineteenth century. It passed to the Cornbrook Brewery and then to Salford brewers Walker & Homfray before closing in 1907. The building was on the corner of Paley Street and Princess Street and the site is now covered by Huntingdon House.

The Railway Hotel in the 1930s

The Peel Hotel shortly after closure

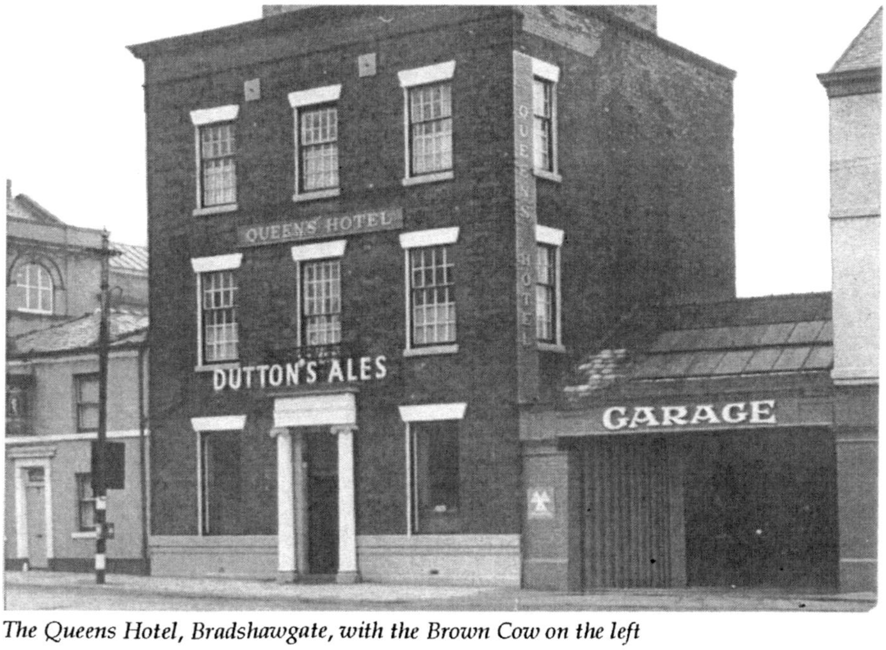

The Queens Hotel, Bradshawgate, with the Brown Cow on the left

Prince of Wales

Pool Street - see Howcroft Inn

Prince of Wales

8 Taylor Street

A Magees beerhouse which stood on the corner of Soho Street and closed in 1915. The site is now covered by Morrisons Supermarket.

Prince William *See Crompton's Mule*

Printers Arms *See New Bridge Inn*

Queen Anne *See Central Hotel*

Queens Arms

42 Bridge Street

The Queens Arms stood next door to the New Market Inn and closed in 1907. It was a beerhouse, previously known as the Flax Tavern, and owned by George Walker's Park View Brewery on Spa Road. The building later became Taylor's pawnshop and partly rebuilt, it is still shop premises.

Queens Arms

131 Deansgate

The Queens Arms was a Sharmans beerhouse which stood on the corner of Queen Street. It closed in 1907 and the site is now occupied by the YMCA and shop premises.

Queens Hotel

155 Bradshawgate

The Queens, owned by the Manchester Brewery Company and sold to Hamers before becoming a Duttons house, was built around 1800, first licensed in 1856 and was on a list of buildings requiring special consideration before being demolished. In his Draft Town Centre Plan (1964), Graeme Shankland suggested that it might be worth preserving. This was not to be; in 1965 both the Queens and the Brown Cow next door closed and were demolished, and on their site rose the Trotters Hotel, opened in 1966.

Quill & Pen *See Donaghy's*

Railway Hotel

17 Trinity Street

This hotel on the corner of Newport Street was a popular resting place for travellers in the heyday of the Bolton railway system, before the Beeching Plan decimated services. The original Railway Tavern was a beerhouse until 1879, when the licence of the Talbot Inn (or Dog), Brown Street, was surrendered in exchange for the granting of a six-day public house licence. In 1935 a full seven-day licence was transferred here from the Cross Keys on Cross Street (see Part Two). The Railway Hotel was a Threlfalls house until 1967, when Whitbread purchased Threlfall-Chesters. The hotel was closed and demolished in 1973 and replaced by a tree-clad, grassed mound providing an open aspect to both Trinity Street and Newport Street. In the mid-1980s the Trinity Street Station clock tower was dismantled and re-erected on the site.

The former John Willie's furniture shop was first licensed in the 1980s and in the early 1990s, when this photograph was taken, it was Chester Moonshines. The premises became the Revolution Bar in 1999

The Red Cross Hotel in the 1920s

Railway Inn

Great Moor Street - see Donaghy's

Railway Shipping Inn

See Brunswick Hotel

Red Cross Hotel

65 Bradshawgate

The Red Cross was first licensed in 1817. In later years it was colloquially known as 't'Blood Tub', owned by Tongs and then Magees when it closed in 1964. The building was demolished in 1968 with adjoining premises Joshua and Tom Taylor (Bolton) Ltd, James Walsh's original jeweller's shop and other property in Silverwell Street. For a time the site was used as a temporary car park until construction of Sun Alliance House, opened in 1971, and Enzo's Restaurant, now Tiggi's.

Red Lion Hotel

48-50 Crook Street

The Red Lion public house opened in the 1840s on the south side of Crook Street, near the Derby Street end. It was owned by William Settle's Rose & Crown Brewery of Cross Street until

1951, when Duttons of Blackburn took over. The pub closed two years later and the site is now part of an extended Trinity Street.

Red on the Square

Nelson Square
A new Thwaites pub which opened in 1999. It covers the site of the old Scholes & Scholes shop and extends into the former Prudential House on the Bradshawgate corner.

Revolution Bar

Bradshawgate
In 1987 the former John Willie's furniture shop became a bar called Carrington's. The name was subsequently changed to Bentley's, then to Chester Moonshines in the 1990s and in 1999 the premises became the Revolution Bar.

Rising Sun *See Imperial Hotel*

Robin Hood

38-40 Ashburner Street
A Sharmans pub on the corner of Spring Gardens which closed in 1928 when the site was acquired by the Corporation. This part of Ashburner Street is now covered by the Museums Department.

Roebuck Hotel

1 Kay Street
The Roebuck opened in the first decade of the nineteenth century and it stood at the corner of Kay Street and Bow Street for over a hundred and fifty years. It was a Tongs house (later Walkers) and closed in 1960 on transfer of its licence to the newly-built Prince Rupert Hotel on Holmeswood Road. The Roebuck was demolished in 1961 and the site is now part of a landscaped area and car park.

The Roebuck in the 1920s

The Robin Hood

The Shepherds Arms in the 1920s

Rotters *See Space City*

Royal Oak *See Prince of Wales, Paley St*

Royal Pavilion *See Villiers Hotel*

Saddle Hotel

48 Bradshawgate
The Saddle Hotel, a Tetley-Walker house, was famous for its 'Saddle pies', a delicacy made on the premises. The hotel closed in 1970 and, along with other buildings between the Pack Horse Hotel and Fold Street, was demolished to make way for the Arndale Centre (now Crompton Place).

The pub dated from the early 1900s, when an older Saddle Hotel was pulled down for the widening of Bradshawgate. The old pub was in existence in the 1790s, when it was known as the Weavers Arms. It is said that it became the Saddle Hotel in the 1840s when the widow of a landlord married a local saddler who changed the name to suit his calling.

St George's Hotel

39-41 St George's Road

The original St George's Hotel opened across from St George's Church in the 1840s. In the 1920s this building and Rothwell's chemist's shop next door, on the corner of Knowsley Street, were demolished and a new semicircular St George's Hotel opened on the site in 1927. The original pub had been a Magees house, but for many years it belonged to Swales Brewery. 'Last orders' were called for the final time in January 1968 and the hostelry was demolished in 1972.

At the same time, all the old properties on the east side of Knowsley Street between the hotel and the River Croal, including Morris's photographer's, Rothwell's chemist's (again), the Scotch Wool and Hosiery Store, Halford's cycle dealers and the NWEB showroom were demolished. The new market place covers the area today.

Same Place Again

9 Independent Street

A Magees beerhouse which closed in 1906 and subsequently became a lodging house. The site is now covered by St Peter's Way.

Sam's Bar
See Crompton's Mule

Scandals *See Academy*

Scotch Vaults *See Bay Horse*

Serendipity's *See Wheatsheaf Hotel*

The Sir Charles Napier in the 1920s

The Lions Paw awaiting demolition. The Silver Vat was built on the site in 1907

Shepherds Arms

44 Kay Street

The Shepherds was a Sharmans beerhouse which closed in 1933. The premises were absorbed into the adjoining Kay Street Mission. The Mission closed in 1958 and was demolished in 1959 for the widening of Kay Street.

Ship Inn

22 Bradshawgate

The Ship Inn, one of Bolton's old licensed houses, was closed and demolished in 1906 for the widening of Bradshawgate and Yates's Wine Lodge was built over part of the site. The Ship was a Magees house in the nineteenth century and shortly before closure it belonged to Wilsons Brewery of Manchester. The licence was transferred to the Sunnyside Hotel on Bloom Street, which was then a beerhouse belonging to Sharmans Brewery.

Silver Vat

75-77 Deansgate

The first pub on this site, on the corner of Old Hall Street North, was the Horse Shoe, later the Four Horse Shoes, which opened in the eighteenth century. For a time it was called the Lions Paw and by 1900 it belonged to the Manchester Brewery Company. They rebuilt the pub in 1907 and called it the Silver Vat, a trade name which they took over with Wingfield's of Nelson Square in 1899. This closed in 1927 and the licence was transferred to one of the Manchester Brewery's beerhouses, the Bowling Green on Bury Road. Parr's Bank, later the National Westminster, was extended over the site of the Silver Vat to occupy the whole area from Oxford Street to Old Hall Street North.

Sir Charles Napier

30 Moor Lane
The Sir Charles Napier was a Sharmans beerhouse which opened in the mid-nineteenth century and closed in 1939. The building erected on the site has had various occupants, latterly Derek's Carpets.

Sir John Falstaff

107-109 Blackhorse Street
A Sharmans beerhouse which closed in 1930. The Falstaff and adjoining property, including Kershaw's Mill and Foundry Square, were pulled down for the building of the Odeon Cinema, which opened in 1937 and became a bingo hall in 1983.

Soho Street Tavern *See Griffin Inn*

Soho Tavern

1 Trinity Street
The Soho Tavern was a Magees beerhouse on the corner of Crook Street. It closed in 1910 and the building was used as a hairdresser's in the 1920s and 1930s. The site is now part of a widened Trinity Street.

The Spinning Mule and Red on the Square

Space City

Howell Croft South
When Elizabeth House opened in 1971 the licensed premises in the basement were called the Va Va Club. This became Rotters Disco in 1978, but closed after a fire a year later. In December 1980 Space City, a pub combined with an electronic games centre, opened there. It subsequently had the name High Society and from 1992, Kiss Night Spot and Fun Bar. The premises re-emerged as Club Liquid in 1997.

Spencer's Bar

See Crown & Cushion

Spinning Mule

Nelson Square
A new pub built by the J D Wetherspoon chain and opened in 1998.

Spread Eagle Hotel

29 Hulme Street
This was a Sharmans public house, opened by 1843 and later owned by Walkers and then Tetley-Walker. It closed in 1981 and the site, at the corner of Lark Street, is now a tree-planted and grassed area.

Star

11 Bow Street
For many years the short stretch of Bow Street boasted four public houses - the New Market Inn on the corner of Bridge Street, the Star & Garter, the Bow Street Tavern and the Roebuck Hotel on the corner of Kay Street. Only the Star, as it is now called, remains today. In the early 1900s it belonged to Sharmans Brewery, passed to Shaws of Leigh and then Walkers of Warrington before becoming a Tetley pub in 1960. In more recent years it was acquired by Vaux Breweries of Sunderland.

Star Inn

Churchgate - see Bush Hotel

Stork Tavern

See Town Hall Hotel

The Spread Eagle Hotel in the 1920s

 Town Centre Pubs 1900-2000

Sun Inn

54 Bradshawgate

The Sun Inn could be traced back to the eighteenth century and from the mid-nineteenth century it was known as Loader's Vaults. The Loaders were wine and spirit merchants and when the Sun closed in 1905 it was owned by a similar firm, Ross, Munro & Company. The building was demolished for the widening of Bradshawgate and the site lies beneath the frontage of Crompton Place.

The Star & Garter (now Star) in the 1920s

Swan Hotel

2-4 Churchgate

The building on Churchgate dates from the early nineteenth century but a Swan Hotel was certainly in existence in the eighteenth century and, it is believed, in the seventeenth century or even earlier. The hotel is linked particularly with trotting (hoaxing), the name from which 'trotter' is given to a Boltonian. The Crown Brewery of Bury were the owners in the early 1920s, followed by Bass, Ratcliff & Gretton of Burton-on-Trent in 1925. There were extensions and alterations in 1930-31, when Hope Brothers and two other shops on the Bradshawgate corner were acquired.

Later owners were Trust Houses Ltd and, in the 1980s, Burtonwood Brewery. There were alterations in 1984-85 and then in 1990 Burtonwood applied to knock the hotel down and replace it with an office block, wine bar and shopping units. The brewers changed their minds and a refurbished Swan opened in July 1992, with Swannies Bar for the 18s to 30s, the Malt & Hops Bar for real ale aficionados and the Buttery Bar for diners. In 1997 the Regent Inns group took over; the Malt & Hops Bar was closed and the public bars were renamed the Cygnet Inn. The latter name disappeared during another renovation in 2000 and in March the real ale bar, styled the Malt & Hops Ale House, reopened.

The Swan Hotel in 1993

The Sweet Green Tavern

Sweet Green Tavern

125-127 Crook Street

If not the first Tetley pub in Bolton, this was certainly one of the first. The Tetley presence in this area derives mainly from the Leeds company's merger with Walkers of Warrington in 1960, but Tetleys acquired the Sweet Green Tavern directly from private owners some years before. The name perpetuates an area which in the early nineteenth century was 'a pleasant place... a place of fragrant gardens and picturesque houses'. From the west door of the church 'a well planted orchard and gardens stretched without intermission to Fletcher Street'. The Sweet Green Tavern was originally a beerhouse and until the extension of

Trinity Street in the late 1960s, it stood on the corner of Soho Street and Crook Street. The pub was redesigned in 1982 and extended into the shop next door.

Sweet Home *See Pineapple Inn*

Temple Tavern

17-19 Dawes Street

This Magees beerhouse stood near the railway bridge on Dawes Street and closed about 1905. The site is now part of the paved area between Morrison's supermarket and the railway bridge.

Three Tuns Hotel

14-16 Bridge Street

The Three Tuns opened in 1808 and closed in November 1956, when the licence was transferred to the Willows Hotel on Willows Lane. The former Magees house was demolished in 1957 and the site is now occupied by part of F W Woolworth & Co's store, opened in March 1959.

Three Tuns

15 Chapel Street

Chapel Street ran from the east side of Kay Street, opposite All Saints Church. The Three Tuns was on the left hand side, approximately three-quarters of the way between Kay Street and Union Street. It was in existence by 1800 and was a Sharmans house before it closed in 1933. The full licence was transferred to the Vulcan beerhouse at Deane. The site of the Three Tuns is now covered by St Peter's Way.

Town Hall Hotel

2 Old Hall Street South

There has often been confusion concerning the Town Hall Tavern and the Town Hall Hotel. The Tavern was sited on Victoria Square and the Town Hall Hotel stood at the corner of Old Hall Street South and Victoria Square. It opened in the 1840s and before Bolton's Town Hall was built it was called the Stork Tavern. Bury's Crown Brewery were the owners when the pub closed in 1933.

The Town Hall Tavern

The premises remained standing until 1947, when they were demolished along with other property on the west side of Old Hall Street. The area to the west was seeded for grass in 1950, and for some considerable time afterwards seats were positioned alongside the plot. The site of the hostelry is approximately at the corner of the present Coronation Street, where the Wellsprings building stands today.

Town Hall Tavern

46-48 Victoria Square

The Tavern was a beerhouse, once owned by Magees and later by Hamers, which closed in 1925. Along with adjoining property, the building was demolished to make way for the Civic Centre. The site now fronts the Magistrates' Courts.

Trotters Hotel

Bradshawgate

The Trotters opened in December 1966,

Victoria Square South and the Town Hall Hotel on the corner of Old Hall Street South, photographed about 1930. Across Old Hall Street South can be seen the Lancashire Wallpaper Co, Leach's health food store and Wood & Co, tea and coffee merchants

replacing two Duttons houses, the Brown Cow and the Queens Hotel, which closed in 1965. After extensive alterations, the pub reopened as the Duck & Firkin in December 1981. It became the Trotters again some years later and, after being closed for a while, was demolished in August 1997. The Ian Anthony showroom on the south corner of Shiffnall Street was built on the site.

Union Arms

41 Ashburner Street

A Magees beerhouse which stood on the corner of Spring Gardens, across from the Robin Hood. It closed in 1925 and the site is now covered by the Lever Chambers Health Centre.

The Varsity

Churchgate

Opened in March 1999 by Wolverhampton & Dudley Breweries on the site of the Boars Head.

Va Va Club *See Space City*

The Varsity

Victoria Buffet

Churchgate

In the late nineteenth century the Victoria Buffet was the public house adjoining the Victoria Theatre of Varieties, the successors to the Museum Music and Concert Hall and the Angel, an old inn which was licensed by the 1770s. In the early twentieth century this enterprise was being run by the Bolton Theatre & Entertainment Company Ltd, who leased the Victoria Buffet to Allsopp's Brewery of Burton-on-Trent.

The Buffet's licence was refused in 1912 and the following year the theatre and Buffet had become the Princess Cinema. This shut in 1928 for extensions to the Theatre Royal, itself closed in 1962 and demolished in 1963. On its site and that of the adjoining Bush Hotel arose a building which, until January 1986, was occupied by a supermarket. The Brasshouse Bar now stands on the site.

Victoria Hotel

17 Hotel Street

The Victoria Hotel opened in the 1840s and is believed to have been the only hotel in Bolton to have enjoyed Royal patronage. In 1876 Prince Arthur, Duke of Connaught, was billeted there whilst accompanying a detachment of the 7th Hussars. From then on the hostelry sported over its doorway the Royal Coat of Arms and a sign on the roof proudly announced 'Under Royal Patronage'. Around that time the hotel was owned by James Hall, a local spirit merchant. The next owners were the Whitefield Brewery Company and when this company was wound up, John Willie Lees of Middleton Junction took over. After that, Hamers of Bromley Cross owned the Victoria and it subsequently became a Duttons house. Mine host for many years was Frank Roberts, Bolton Wanderers, Manchester City and England forward.

The Victoria closed in 1961 and was demolished along with adjoining property including Stanley Haywood's chemist's and Naylor's tobacco and sweets shop to make way for the third extension of Marks & Spencer's store, opened in June 1968.

The Three Tuns in the 1920s

Villiers Hotel

26 Bank Street

In the late eighteenth and nineteenth centuries this was the Hare & Hounds. It became a Tongs Brewery house and was later in the hands of the Whitefield Brewery Company. When this company was wound up, J W Lees of Middleton Junction had the hotel for a time, but it was closed in 1911 for being 'ill conducted'.

The building became a lodging house and then in 1963 opened as the Beachcomber Coffee Bar and Disco. Later it was the Cromwellian Club, then part of Playmate; Maxwell's Plum in 1977 and in 1990 the Royal Pavilion. There was another change in 1996 to Hero's Fun Pub.

Volunteer Inn *See Empire Lounge*

Vulcan Inn

130 Great Moor Street

The Vulcan Inn, at the corner of Great Moor Street and Crook Street, opened as a beerhouse and became fully licensed in 1874, when the Angel & Woolpack on Deansgate (see Part Three) was pulled down and the licence was transferred here. In the late nineteenth century the Vulcan was a Magees house, then it was owned by the Manchester Brewery Company, Walker & Homfray and finally, from 1949, Wilsons Brewery. The pub closed in 1973 and the site is now part of the extended Trinity Street.

The Vulcan in 1961

Waggon & Horses

84 Moor Lane

This was a Manchester Brewery Company beerhouse (earlier Wingfields) which closed in 1903. It stood on the corner of Back Partridge Street and the property was pulled down for the widening of the Lancashire & Yorkshire Railway Company's line.

Weavers Arms *See Saddle Hotel*

Welcome Home

124 Deansgate

The licence of this beerhouse lapsed in 1900 and the building was demolished for a Deansgate widening scheme. Like the nearby Bee Hive, it was a J G Swales house. The Head Post Office was erected on part of the site in 1913-1916.

Welcome Traveller *See Wellington*

The White Lion in the 1950s

Wellington Inn

11 Union Buildings, Bradshawgate

In the mid-nineteenth century this beerhouse was called the Welcome Traveller. It was located across from the present Anchor Inn and closed in 1906, when it belonged to Hamers Volunteer Brewery of Bromley Cross.

Wheatsheaf Hotel

50 Great Moor Street

An earlier Wheatsheaf opened in 1810 and stood near to the entrance to the Unitarian Church on 'Windy Bank' (Bank Street). This was demolished and its licence was transferred to newly-built premises at the corner of Great Moor Street and Newport Street in 1835.

In the 1880s and 1890s the licensee of the Wheatsheaf was George Walker, proprietor of the Bolton Brewery Company Ltd (later the Spa Wells Brewery). Magees later acquired the pub and the old 'round house' building was demolished in 1962. The first portion of a new Wheatsheaf, set further back than its predecessor, was opened in November of that year. There were major alterations by Greenall Whitley in 1986, when the pub reopened as Serendipity's. After a long period of closure in the 1990s, the building was converted into the Home Bargains Store in 1997/98.

White Horse Hotel

Mealhouse Lane

The White Horse was an alehouse dating from the eighteenth century which closed in 1901. It was on the corner of Ship Gates and was one of several properties acquired for extensions to the Bolton Evening News offices, completed in 1907.

White Lion

169-171 Deansgate

The White Lion dates from the end of the eighteenth century. At the beginning of the twentieth it was owned by the Manchester Brewery Company and it became a Wilsons pub in 1949. The building, once threatened with demolition, was given a costly renovation in 1985. The owners in 2000 are the Unique Pub Company.

White Swan

3 Deane Road

The White Swan was a Cornbrook Brewery beerhouse which stood on the corner of Moor Lane and Deane Road and closed in 1908. It was next door to the Milestone Hotel and the site is now fronting a grassed area alongside Bolton Institute's Deane Campus.

Winston's

See Gipsy's Tent

Woodmans Cottage

2 Deane Road

The Woodmans Cottage was the first building on the right hand side of Deane Road. It was a beerhouse and belonged to the Openshaw Brewery of West Gorton, Manchester, before it closed in 1959. The site lies between the Moor Lane Fire Station and a car parking area.

The three-storey York Hotel in the 1970s

(Old) Woolpack

25 Deansgate

The Woolpack was an eighteenth-century licensed house on the corner of Mealhouse Lane and it was a Tongs house when it closed in 1911. The site is now occupied by the HSBC Bank.

Yates's Wine Lodge, photographed shortly before the premises were extended into the building on the left

Yates's Wine Lodge

Bradshawgate

In 1890 Yates Brothers acquired the eighteenth century Bulls Head on Bradshawgate, part of the estate of the Earl of Bradford, and this became their fifth wine lodge in the country. The present terra cotta premises were constructed in 1906. There was a major facelift in 1984 and in 1998 the premises were greatly enlarged when the adjoining building which once housed the Burnley Building Society was taken over.

York Hotel

112-114 Newport Street

The York dates from before 1850 and for many years in the nineteenth century the pub was owned and run by the Hardcastle family. It subsequently became a Magees house and then passed to the present owners, Burtonwood Brewery. In 1985 the York was one of a select band of public houses throughout the whole of England to have been named in all twelve of CAMRA's Good Beer Guides. Extensive alterations and renovations in that year included the removal of the top storey and the pub reopened in January 1986.

Part Two

PUBS OUTSIDE THE TOWN CENTRE 1900-2000

The following list contains all the twentieth century public houses and beerhouses in the Bolton licensing area beyond the town centre, but excluding districts such as Astley Bridge, Deane and Great Lever. The addresses are those given in the Post Office 1896-1898 directory. Details of ownership and most closure dates are taken from licensing records.

African Chief

7 Moss Street

A beerhouse owned by Charles Seddon of the St George's Hotel, St George's Road, in the 1860s. Later owners included Atkinson's (Commission Street Brewery), the Cornbrook Brewery and finally Hamers. The licence was refused in May 1908.

Ainsworth Arms

606 Halliwell Road

A former Tongs Brewery pub.

Albert Inn

181 Derby Street

In the 1870s this was owned by brewer James Leach, whose brewery was behind the pub. Cunningham's Brewery of Warrington later acquired the Albert and in 1951 it was one of several they sold to Tetleys of Leeds.

Albert Inn

46-48 Poplar Street

A former Tongs beerhouse which closed in 1952.

Albert Inn

30 Progress Street

A Magees beerhouse whose licence was surrendered in 1901 in exchange for an off-licence.

The Arrowsmiths Arms in the 1920s

Alexandra Hotel

14 Stewart Street

This beerhouse was adjacent to Halliwell's Alexandra Brewery and it became a Magees house in 1910 when the Alexandra Brewery closed. It became a public house in early 1935 when the Four Factories on Turton Street closed and the licence was transferred here. The Alexandra lasted only a few more months and closed the same year.

Alfred the Great

44 Noble Street

A beerhouse owned by the licensee, Joseph Atkinson, from the 1860s to the 1890s, then by Settle's Rose & Crown Brewery and then Duttons. A full licence was acquired in 1961 and the pub closed in 1964.

Anchor Inn

15 Bury Old Road

A former Magees beerhouse, earlier known as the Bright View. Today it is a free house selling Bass beers.

Archduke Charles *See The Duke*

Arrowsmiths Arms

35 Mill Street

Opened as a beerhouse in the 1830s and a fully licensed house by 1849. It later became a Sharmans pub and closed in 1933. The licence was transferred to the King William IV on Manchester Road. (See Greengate Inn)

Bank View Inn

66-68 Kestor Street

A former home-brew beerhouse which

The Ainsworth Arms in the 1920s

was owned by Sharmans when it closed in 1937.

Bedrock Cafe *See Tippings Arms*

Bee Hive Inn

51-53 Back Derby Street
A Magees beerhouse which closed in 1936.

Belle Vue

224 Halliwell Road
This was a beerhouse owned by Samuel Smith of the Dog & Snipe Brewery, Folds Road, and was later acquired by John Smiths of Tadcaster. A full licence was granted in 1960.

Black Dog

82 Halliwell Road
A former Magees beerhouse which closed in 1984.

Black Horse

261 Derby Street
Owned by Thomas Iddon of the Prince of Wales Hotel, Mount Street, in the 1870s. It was later acquired by Wingfields Silverwell Brewery and then the Manchester Brewery Company. There was an objection to the licence in May 1914, but the beerhouse managed to stay in business until 1917.

Black Horse

91 Kay Street
A Sharmans beerhouse, closed in 1901.

The Albert Inn, Poplar Street, in the 1920s

Black Lion

18 Turton Street
A beerhouse owned by Atkinsons and later the Cornbrook Brewery. It closed in 1913.

The Bank View Inn in the 1920s

Blue Bell

145 Kay Street
A beerhouse which belonged to Halliwell's Alexandra Brewery and then Magees. It closed in 1933.

Boilermakers Arms

48 Phoenix Street
One of a handful of Bolton beerhouses owned by the Crown Brewing Company of Bury. It closed in 1956.

Borough Arms

108 Higher Bridge Street
A Sharmans, then Peter Walker beerhouse which became fully licensed in 1961 and closed in the 1990s.

Bowling Green

138-140 Blackburn Road
Once a home-brew pub, then a Sharmans, later a Walkers house.

Bowling Green

97 Eskrick Street
A former Magees pub.

Bradford Arms

28 Foundry Street
A Hamers, later Duttons beerhouse which closed about 1960.

Bradford Hotel

107 Bradford Street
A beerhouse until 1880, when the licence from the White Bear on Deansgate (see Part Three) was transferred here. It was owned by Tongs, then Walkers and is now a Tetley pub.

Brewers Arms
4 Atherton Street
A beerhouse which belonged to the Phoenix Brewery of Heywood, then Wingfields Silverwell Brewery and finally the Manchester Brewery Company. It closed in 1924.

Bricklayers Arms
See Houghton Street Tavern

Bridge Tavern
See Lever Bridge Inn

Bridgeman Arms
81 Bridgeman Street
This was listed as a public house from about 1825 until the 1840s, then later as a beerhouse. It was owned by Atkinsons Brewery, then Magees, and closed in 1960.

Bright View
See Anchor Inn

British Oak
212 Derby Street
In the 1870s this beerhouse was owned by Joseph Atkinson, licensee of the Alfred the Great, Noble Street. The next owner was brewer W T Settle and the British Oak subsequently became a Duttons house. A full licence was acquired in 1961 and the pub closed a few years later.

British Queen
See Old Original British Queen

Buck & Vine
142 Kay Street
A Wilsons beerhouse which closed in 1960.

The Buxton Arms in the 1920s

Buxton Arms
37-39 Buxton Street
From the 1870s the owner of this beerhouse was listed as Ellen Ashton, who was also the owner and licensee of the Robin Hood on Ashburner Street. Sharmans Brewery took over and the Buxton Arms was a Walkers pub when it closed in 1964.

Caledonian
1-3 Lyon Street
Robert Wood & Sons of the Prince Arthur Brewery owned this beerhouse in the late nineteenth century. It became a Tongs, then a Walkers house and closed in the 1960s.

The Bowling Green, Blackburn Road, in the 1920s

Carringtons *See White Hart*

Cattle Market
6 Orlando Street
Originally the Spotted Cow, the Cattle Market was one of the Earl of Bradford's Bolton properties before becoming a Threlfalls and then a Whitbread house.

Cattle Market Tavern
38 Foundry Street
A beerhouse owned by James Leach of the Albert Brewery. The licence was refused in 1909.

Church Inn
45-47 Bamber Street
A Tongs beerhouse at the beginning of the twentieth century, the Church was subsequently leased by Hydes Brewery of Manchester for about ten years. It became a Burtonwood house, was fully licensed in 1961 and closed about 1970.

Church Inn
106 Folds Road
A Sharmans, later Walkers beerhouse which closed in 1969.

Churchills *See Rose Hill*

City Hotel
39 Eskrick Street
A home-brew beerhouse at the end of the nineteenth century which became fully licensed in 1961. It was a Groves & Whitnall (Salford) house and was rebuilt in 1968.

Claremont Hotel *See Great Eastern*

Coe Street Tavern

52 Coe Street
A beerhouse owned by Atkinsons Brewery and later Cornbrook Brewery. It closed in 1949.

Constitution Arms

See Duke of Connaught

Corn Mill Tavern

120 Blackburn Road
A beerhouse which closed in 1906 when Sharmans Brewery gave up the licence as part of a deal to obtain a full licence for the Sunnyside Hotel on Bloom Street.

Corporation

58-60 Mason Street
A Tongs, later Walkers beerhouse which closed in the 1960s.

Cottage

58 Cannon Street
In the 1880s this beerhouse was owned by Henry Greenwood, a brewer in Crown Street and proprietor of the Swan Hotel, Churchgate. It passed to Wingfields Brewery and then to the Manchester Brewery Company. The Cottage closed in 1959.

Cotton Tree

60 Lever Street
A beerhouse owned by Atkinsons and later the Cornbrook Brewery and then Magees. It closed in 1962.

Craddock Arms

63 Craddock Street
A beerhouse owned by Atkinsons and later the Cornbrook Brewery. It closed in 1968.

Craven Heifer

75 Derby Street
In the late nineteenth century this beerhouse was owned by Joseph Atkinson, licensee of the Alfred the Great, Noble Street. It became a Magees house and closed in 1912.

The Crofters Hotel, St George's Road, in the early twentieth century

The Cattle Market, Orlando Street, in the 1930s

The Bradford Hotel, Bradford Street, in the 1920s

Crawford Arms

19 Bolton Street
A Hamers and then Duttons beerhouse which became fully licensed in 1961 and closed in 1979.

Cricketers Arms

33-35 Hibbert Street
Originally a beerhouse, the Cricketers became a public house in 1874 when the licence of the Millstone, Deansgate (see Part Three), was transferred here. The owner then was the licensee, William Lee, and the pub subsequently became a Threlfalls house. It was later owned by Whitbread and closed in the 1990s.

Crofters

494 Halliwell Road
A pub which brewed its own beer in

the nineteenth century and in the twentieth was leased by several breweries, including Cornbrook, Burtonwood and Magees.

Crofters Hotel

St George's Road
An old public house, sometimes listed as the Whitsters Arms, which was first licensed about 1800. In the 1870s the property was owned by James Deakin of the Manchester Brewery Company, then it was acquired by Bolton Corporation, who subsequently sold it to Magees. In 1906/7 the brewery rebuilt the pub and as part of the deal the licence of the New Bridge Inn, was given up and Magees paid the Corporation £500. In later years the name of the pub was changed to Magees. After a period of closure in the 1990s it reopened with a new licence as Gallaghers Oyster Bar and in March 2000 it was advertised as the Oystercatcher Brasserie Bar.

Cromptons Monument

39 Mill Street
A beerhouse which belonged to Atkinsons and later the Cornbrook Brewery. A full licence was granted in 1961 and the pub closed in 1972.

Cross Guns

272 Deane Road
A former Tongs and then Walkers pub.

Cross Keys

Cross Street
A fully licensed house which was in existence by 1800 and in later years belonged to Tongs and then Hamers Brewery. It closed in 1935, when the licence was transferred to the Railway Hotel on Trinity Street.

The Corporation, Mason Street, in the 1920s

Crown Hotel

213 Derby Street
Owned by David Magee, founder of the nearby Crown Brewery, and a Magees house until it closed in 1980.

Crown Hotel

172 Folds Road
Opened in the 1840s, this was later a Tongs, then a Walkers public house and it closed in 1969.

Derby Arms

98 Derby Street
Originally a beerhouse, the Derby Arms became fully licensed in 1875

The Church Inn, Folds Road, in the 1920s

when it was given the licence of the Horse & Jockey on Bradshawgate (see Part Three). Twentieth century owners included Magees, Duttons and Whitbread, and it subsequently sold Burtonwood beers.

Derby Hotel

218 Halliwell Road

Once a home-brew beerhouse, the Derby became a Sharmans and later a Walkers pub. It got its full licence in 1962 and since the 1980s has been called the Sharman Arms.

Dog & Snipe

181 Folds Road

Brewer Samuel Smith was based here in the latter part of the nineteenth century. The beerhouse was later a Hamers and then a Duttons house. It gained a full licence in 1961 and closed in 1973.

The Duke

Deane Road

Originally the Archduke, or Archduke Charles, this public house dated from the late eighteenth century. It still had its own brewery at the end of the nineteenth century, was later owned by Tongs and then Walkers and eventually closed in the 1990s.

Duke of Bolton

70 Folds Road

In the 1870s this beerhouse was owned by Ellis Marshall of the One Horseshoe, Manor Street. It had become a Magee Marshall house by the time it closed in 1912.

Duke of Connaught

85 Mill Street

Originally the Constitution Arms, this beerhouse was owned by Magees until it shut in 1965.

The Cricketers in the 1950s

Duke of Wellington

26 John Street

An Atkinsons and later Cornbrook beerhouse which had its licence refused in 1905.

Egerton Arms

284 Lever Street

A beerhouse which was owned by Henry Heyes of the Fox Brewery (Fox & Goose beerhouse), 1[illegible]0 Deansgate (see Part Three), in the 1870s. The next owners were the Grants Tower Brewery Company of Ewood Bridge. It was a Cornbrook house when it closed in 1962.

Elephant & Castle

103 Kay Street

A Sharmans beerhouse which closed in 1921.

Falcon Hotel

90 Kay Street

Opened in 1803, the Falcon was a

The Cross Guns in the 1920s

Tongs and later a Walkers pub. It belonged to Tetleys when it closed in 1986.

Farmers Arms

205 Bridgeman Street

A public house owned by licensee James Ramwell in the 1870s. By 1900 it was owned by George Munro & Co, wine and spirit merchants of Deansgate. The next owners were listed as Swan's Vintage Wine Stores Ltd of Preston, then Thomas L Robinson, also of Preston. The pub closed in the 1970s.

The Farmers Arms, Bridgeman Street, awaiting demolition in the 1970s

Farmers Arms

86-88 Chorley Street

This Greenalls pub was for many years a Magees beerhouse and it became fully licensed in 1962.

Farmers Arms

251 Derby Street

A home-brew beerhouse in the nineteenth century and later owned by Hamers and then Duttons. A full licence was granted in 1961.

Farmers Arms

Lever Street - see Tanners Arms

Foresters Arms

63 Smith Street

In the late nineteenth century this beerhouse was owned by Thomas Holden of the Lord Clyde on Folds Road. The Bury Brewery Company were the owners when the licence was refused in 1911.

Derby Hotel, Halliwell Road, in the 1920s

Foresters Arms

45 Union Street

A beerhouse which belonged to Atkinsons and later the Cornbrook Brewery. It nearly lost its licence in 1900 when the tenant was convicted of running a disorderly house, but there was an appeal and the Foresters survived until 1934.

The Falcon in the 1920s

Forge Tavern

219-221 Bridgeman Street

A Magees beerhouse which closed about 1960.

Fountain Inn

32 Nelson Street

A beerhouse owned by Robert Wood of the Prince Arthur Brewery and for a time a Magees house. It closed in 1930.

Four Factories

34 Turton Street

A public house opened about 1808 and later owned by the Alexandra Brewery. When it closed in 1935 the licence was transferred to the Alexandra Hotel.

Fox Tavern

23 Emmanuel Street

A home-brew beerhouse which seems

to have had a variety of owners, including Sharmans Brewery, Thomas Sherrington of the Bull & Wharf and Chadwicks Walmersley Brewery of Bury. The Fox closed in 1919.

Fox & Stork *See Stork*

Gallaghers *See Crofters Hotel*

Gasworks Tavern
91 Mill Street
A Sharmans, later Wingfields and then Manchester Brewery beerhouse which closed in 1935.

General Havelock
110 Sidney Street
A home-brew beerhouse in the late nineteenth century, owned by a Mrs Mahalah Hardcastle, who ran the York Hotel, Newport Street, from the 1860s to the 1880s. The General Havelock was acquired by the Openshaw Brewery of Manchester and was a Bass house when it closed in the1980s.

Gibraltar Rock
244 Deane Road
A public house opened as the Gibraltar Tavern in 1806. In the 1880s it was owned by Mrs Elizabeth Rostron of the Old Bridge Inn on Bridge Street, who also owned the Founders Arms on St George's Street. The Gibraltar Rock subsequently became a Magees house.

Gilnow Arms
256-258 Deane Road
A Tongs, then Walkers beerhouse which became fully licensed in 1961.

Gladstone Hotel
73-75 Deane Road
A Magees beerhouse, formerly known as the Returned Sailor, which closed in the 1960s.

The Globe Inn in the 1960s

Globe Inn
76 Higher Bridge Street
A beerhouse which belonged to Wingfields Brewery, then to the Manchester Brewery Company and later Wilsons. It became fully licensed in 1961.

The Greengate Inn in the 1920s

Golden Cup
12 Haigh Street
In the 1880s this beerhouse belonged to John Tong, a provision dealer and beer retailer of Dixon Green, Farnworth. It subsequently became a Walkers house and closed in 1959.

Golden Lion *See Kay Street Arms*

Good Samaritan
73 Derby Street
A Magees beerhouse which closed in 1969.

Great Eastern
288 Waterloo Street
A beerhouse which belonged to the Alexandra Brewery and then Magees. It was originally called the Claremont Hotel and stood at number 221 Waterloo Street. In 1883 permission was given to transfer the licence to a building on the other side of the street. This closed in 1968.

Greengate Inn
19-21 Hammond Street
A beerhouse which was owned by Robert Wood of the Prince Arthur Brewery and later by Tongs. In 1933 this licence, along with the licences of the Masons Arms on Emblem Street, the Merehall Inn on Lyon Street and the Black Horse, St Johns Road (Chew Moor), were surrendered in a deal

which allowed the transfer of the full licences of the Old Robin Hood (Lever Street), the Three Tuns (Chapel Street) and the Arrowsmiths Arms (Mill Street) to the Nightingale, the Vulcan (Deane) and the King William IV respectively.

Greens Arms

25 St Helens Road

A beerhouse which was owned by Fairhurst's Brewery of Wigan, then Magees and closed about 1970.

Grey Mare

50 Turton Street

A Magees beerhouse whose licence was given up in 1906 in exchange for an off licence.

Half Way House

127-129 Derby Street

A Magees beerhouse which closed about 1970.

Halliwell Lodge

Mornington Road

A hotel which opened in 1899 with the licence of the Rope & Anchor, Deansgate (see Part Three), and closed in the 1980s.

Hark up to Glory

See Noble Street Tavern

The Crown Hotel, Folds Road, in the 1920s

Haydock Arms

28-30 Haydock Street

A beerhouse which belonged to the Alexandra Brewery, then Magees and closed in 1950.

Hearts of Oak

63 Haydock Street

A beerhouse which was owned by Hydes Brewery of Manchester in the early twentieth century and then by Burtonwood. It closed in 1959.

The Fountain Inn, Nelson Street, in the 1920s

Horse and Vulcan

59-61 Deane Road

A home-brew beerhouse, later owned by Sharmans and closed in 1912.

Houghton Street Tavern

34 Houghton Street

A beerhouse, which in 1876 was listed as the Bricklayers Arms. It was owned by Leach's Albert Brewery and then Tetleys of Leeds. It became fully licensed in 1961 and closed in the 1970s.

John Bull Inn

5 Bamber Street

A beerhouse owned by Atkinsons and then Cornbrook Brewery. The licence was refused in 1901 because it was a disorderly house.

Jolly Angler

74-76 Hulme Street

In the nineteenth century this beerhouse was owned by Mrs Mahalah Hardcastle of the York Hotel, Newport Street. It seems to have remained in private hands until closure in 1919.

Jolly Carter

279-281 Derby Street

A beerhouse owned by Atkinson's Commission Street Brewery and then Magees. The licence was one of three surrendered in 1904 so that the Pike View could become fully licensed.

Jolly Waggoner

346 Deane Road
Originally a Magees beerhouse which became fully licensed in 1960.

Junction Inn

77-79 Egyptian Street
Once called the Smoothing Iron, this beerhouse belonged to the Alexandra Brewery and was a Magees house when it closed in the 1960s.

Kay Street Arms

159 Kay Street
Formerly called the Golden Lion. Among the early owners of this beerhouse were Atkinsons and the Alexandra Brewery. It was a Magees house when it closed in 1966.

Kings Arms

177 Chorley Old Road
A beerhouse owned by Robert Wood of the Prince Arthur Brewery and then Tongs and Walkers. It became fully licensed in 1934 when the Imperial Hotel on Church Bank closed.

King William IV

202 Manchester Road
A beerhouse with its own brewery which later became a Tongs house. It received a full licence from the Arrowsmiths Arms in 1933. The pub closed in 1999 and the building is now business premises.

Lamb Inn

276 Halliwell Road
A former Magees pub, later Greenalls.

The Lord Nelson in the 1920s

Lark Hill Tavern

227 St George's Road
A Magees beerhouse, closed in 1926.

Lever Bridge Inn

208-210 Radcliffe Road
Originally a beerhouse, listed as the Bridge Tavern in 1849. In the 1890s it was owned by Messrs Horridge & Co, bleachers, and was later acquired by Tetleys of Leeds. More recently it became a Vaux house.

Little John

184 Lever Street
A beerhouse belonging to the Prince Arthur Brewery, then Tongs and later Walkers. It became fully licensed in 1962.

Lodge Bank Tavern

262-264 Bridgeman Street
A beerhouse with its own brewery in the nineteenth century. It was owned by Samuel Smith of the Dog & Snipe Brewery and then J G Swales of Hulme, Manchester. This company was taken over by Boddingtons, who sold the Lodge Bank to its present owners, J W Lees of Middleton Junction.

Lord Ashley

29 Tyndall Street
A beerhouse belonging to Halliwell's Alexandra Brewery, then Magees. It had closed by the 1950s.

Lord Byron

58-60 Sidney Street
In the 1870s this beerhouse was owned by Mrs Ann Cooper, licensee of the Star & Garter, Bow Street. Several breweries later had an interest in the property, including Magees, Wingfields, the Manchester Brewery and the Alexandra Brewery. When it closed in 1915, James Jackson & Sons of the Spa Road Brewery were the lessees.

The Little John in the 1920s

Lord Clyde

107-109 Folds Road

A home-brew beerhouse in the late nineteenth century and owned by the licensee, Thomas Holden. It was acquired by Atkinson's Commission Street Brewery and was later a Cornbrook and then a Bass house. The full licence was granted in 1961 and in 1991 the pub was bought by Hydes of Manchester.

Lord Hill

46 Sidney Street

In the 1870s this beerhouse belonged to Ellis Crompton, who had a brewery on Derby Street. The next owners were Atkinsons Brewery and it was a Cornbrook house when it closed in 1951.

Lord Napier

141-143 Bridgeman Street

Listed as Shakespeare Tavern in 1876. John Ward, licensee of the Fleece Inn, Bradshawgate, was the owner in the 1860s, then it became an Atkinsons house and was owned by Cornbrook when it closed in 1915.

Lord Nelson

119-121 Derby Street

This was one of the oldest pubs on Derby Street and was in existence by 1800. It was later a Sharmans house and belonged to Walkers when it closed in 1966.

Lord Raglan

384 Halliwell Road

A beerhouse with its own brewery which was still in production in the 1930s. It was owned by Hamers, then Duttons before becoming a Whitbread house. A full licence was granted in 1961.

The Mitre Inn in the 1930s

Magees *See Crofters Hotel*

Masons Arms

45-47 Emblem Street

A beerhouse owned by Joseph Atkinson, who ran the Alfred the Great on Noble Street from the 1860s. Sharmans were the owners when the licence was surrendered in 1933. (See Greengate Inn.)

Masons Arms

125-127 Turton Street

A beerhouse which belonged to the Alexandra Brewery and then Magees. The licence was surrendered in 1913 in exchange for a beer off-licence.

Merehall Inn

2-4 Lyon Street

In the 1880s this was owned by George Walker, proprietor of the Park View Brewery, Spa Road. James Jackson & Sons later owned the brewery and the beerhouse was eventually acquired by Shaws of Leigh when they took over in 1927. The licence was surrendered in 1933. (See Greengate Inn)

Middleton Arms

27 Charles Street

A beerhouse owned by the Bedford Brewing & Malting Company of Leigh, the predecessor of Shaws Brewery. The licence was refused in 1906.

Mill Hill Tavern

121-123 Mill Hill Street

A beerhouse which was owned by Henry Heyes of the Fox Brewery (Fox

The Masons Arms, Emblem Street, in the 1920s

& Goose beerhouse), 160 Deansgate (see Part Three), in the 1870s. The next owners were Magees and then the Grants Tower Brewery Company of Ewood Bridge. It was later a Tongs, then a Walkers house and acquired a full licence in 1962. The pub closed in 1972.

Mitre Inn

55 Haworth Street

A beerhouse owned by the Empress Brewery of Manchester and then Walkers. It closed in 1967.

Mortfield Tavern

18 Gaskell Street

A beerhouse owned by Robert Wood of the Prince Arthur Brewery and later by Tongs and then Walkers. The licence was surrendered in 1957, along with that of the Bee Hive, Duke Street, in an agreement which involved the transfer of the licence of the Pineapple on Radcliffe Road, Darcy Lever, to the new Castle Hotel on Crompton Way.

Mount Pleasant Inn

44-46 Mill Street

A Sharmans beerhouse which had its licence refused in 1913.

Mount Street Inn

136 Mount Street

A Sharmans, later Walkers beerhouse which was fully licensed in 1961 but closed a few years later.

Nailmakers Arms

65-67 Folds Road

A beerhouse that was owned by Seeds Brewery of Radcliffe and later Tongs. It closed in 1912.

The Mount Street Inn in the 1920s

Napier Tavern

149 Deane Road

A Wingfields beerhouse later owned by the Manchester Brewery and Walker & Homfray of Salford. It closed in 1940.

Nelson Arms

11 Nelson Street

A beerhouse which was first listed as the Spinners Arms. It was owned by Joseph Atkinson of the Alfred the Great, Noble Street, in the latter part of the nineteenth century and later by Joseph Stocks & Co Ltd of the Shibden Head Brewery, Halifax. It closed in 1943.

Nelson Hotel

30 Chorley Old Road

A Sharmans, then Walkers beerhouse which became fully licensed in 1961.

Nelsons Monument

65 Blackburn Road

A beerhouse owned by Atkinsons and then Cornbrook Brewery which closed in 1938.

New Cabin *See Uncle Tom's Cabin*

New Inn

45 Coe Street

A home-brew beerhouse which in the 1870s was owned by Joseph Mangnall, the licensee. Wilsons Brewery were the owners in the twentieth century and the New Inn closed in 1960.

New Inn

34 Halliwell Road

A Cornbrook beerhouse which became a Bass house and was fully licensed in 1961.

Nightingale Inn

93-95 Lever Street

A Tongs and then Walkers beerhouse which became fully licensed in 1933 when the Old Robin Hood on the other

The Mortfield Tavern in the 1920s

side of the street closed. (See Greengate Inn) The Nightingale closed in 1998.

Ninehouse Tavern

27 Ninehouse Lane

A Tongs beerhouse which became fully licensed in 1934 when the Sir Sidney Smith closed. The Ninehouse closed in the 1970s.

Noble Street Tavern

85-87 Noble Street

A beerhouse, once called the Hark up to Glory, which was owned by Robert Wood of the Prince Arthur Brewery. The licence was refused in 1906.

Norfolk Arms *See Prince Hotel*

Oddfellows Arms

140 St Helens Road

This was originally a Magees beerhouse. In 1894 the rebuilt Oddfellows was given the licence from the Lord Collingwood on Deansgate (see Part Three) when that pub closed.

Old House at Home

20-22 Kirkhall Lane

A Tongs beerhouse which closed in 1934.

Old Original British Queen

107 Blackburn Road

In the 1840s this was a beerhouse called the British Queen. The Victoria British Queen opened across the road and so the name was changed. It was later a Hamers, then a Duttons house and became fully licensed in 1961. It subsequently became a Whitbread pub.

The New Inn, Coe Street, in the 1960s

Old Vulcan

13-15 Croasdale Street

A Magees and later a Burtonwood beerhouse which closed in the 1960s.

Oliver Cromwell

125 Bridgeman Street

A Magees beerhouse whose licence was surrendered in 1962, along with that of the Peels Arms on Sidney Street, when Magees obtained a new licence for the Morris Dancers on Morris Green Lane.

The Ninehouse Tavern in the 1920s

Oxnoble Inn

67 Bridgeman Street

A beerhouse which originally had its own brewery and was later owned by Atkinsons and then the Cornbrook Brewery. It closed in 1960.

Park Hotel

259 Bridgeman Street

This was a beerhouse until 1873, when it received the full licence of the Three Arrows, Old Hall Street (see Part Three). The Park belonged to Sharmans before becoming a Walkers and then a Tetley pub.

Peacock Arms

72 Kay Street

An Atkinsons and later Cornbrook beerhouse which closed in 1911.

Peels Arms

423 Halliwell Road

Originally a beerhouse, the Peels Arms belonged to Wingfield's Silverwell Brewery and the Manchester Brewery Company before becoming a Wilsons house in 1949. It gained a full licence in 1961.

Peels Arms

30 Sidney Street

A Magees beerhouse whose licence was surrendered in 1962, along with that of the Oliver Cromwell on Bridgeman Street, when Magees obtained a new licence for the Morris Dancers on Morris Green Lane.

Peels Arms

82 Waterloo Street

A Tongs and then Walkers beerhouse which was fully licensed in 1961 and closed a few years later.

Phoenix Tavern

12 Phoenix Street

A beerhouse owned by Seeds Brewery of Radcliffe, then Tongs. It closed in 1913.

Pike View

321 Derby Street

A beerhouse which in the 1870s was owned by Robert Dobson, wholesale brewer of the Parkfield Inn, Crook Street. It was later a Magees house and became fully licensed in 1904, when three licences were surrendered: the Elephant & Castle on Blackhorse Street, the Jolly Carter on Derby Street and a beer off-licence at 68-70 Rosamond Street.

Pilkington Arms

152 Derby Street

A public house which was opened in 1806 by John Pilkington, hence the name. It was later owned by George Walker of the Park View Brewery, Spa Road, then Shaws and then Walkers before becoming a Tetley house.

The Peels Arms, Halliwell Road, in 1961

Pineapple

117 Bridgeman Street

A beerhouse belonging to Wingfields Brewery and then the Manchester Brewery Company. The licence was refused in 1903 because it was a disorderly house, but an appeal was allowed and the Pineapple survived until 1936.

Poplar Inn

74 Kent Street

A beerhouse owned by Wingfields, the Manchester Brewery and then Wilsons. It closed in the 1970s.

Portland Hotel

28 Portland Street

This public house opened in 1880 when it received the licence from the Antelopes Head (see Part Three) on Churchgate. It was a Sharmans, then a Walkers and latterly a Tetley house. It closed in the 1980s.

The Park Hotel, Bridgeman Street, in the 1920s

Premier Arms

38-40 Hulme Street

A Hamers beerhouse, closed in 1920.

Prince Hotel

30 Thwaites Street

A beerhouse, originally called the Norfolk Arms, which belonged to Robert Wood of the Prince Arthur Brewery. It was a Tongs house when it closed in 1935.

Prince Alfred

32 Smith Street

In the late nineteenth century this beerhouse was owned by Herbert Rostron, licensee of the Union Arms, Bullock Street. Later owners included the Alexandra Brewery, Magees and James Jackson of the Spa Road Brewery. It closed in 1918.

Prince Arthur

82 St John Street

A beerhouse owned by brewer Robert Wood and later by Tongs and Walkers. It closed in the 1970s.

Prince of Wales

102 Mount Street

A public house owned by Wingfields, then by the Manchester Brewery Company. It was a Wilsons house when it closed in 1965.

Queen Elizabeth

230 Fletcher Street

Originally a Magees beerhouse, this became a public house in 1875 when it received the licence from the

Wellington Inn on Garside Street (see Part Three).

Queens Hotel

6-8 Darley Street

A Magees beerhouse which closed in the 1960s.

Railway Inn

273 Bridgeman Street

A Magees beerhouse which closed in 1964.

Railway Hotel

2 St Helens Road

Originally a beerhouse, the full licence was transferred from the Rose & Crown, Deansgate, in 1884 (see Part Three). In later years the Railway was a Whitbread pub and for a time before it closed in the 1990s was known as the Shamrock Bar.

Rainforth Hotel

58 School Hill

A Tongs and later Walkers beerhouse which closed in 1959.

Rams Head

275 Derby Street

A beerhouse which opened in the 1830s and was fully licensed by 1843. It was owned by Magees and later Greenalls and closed in 1987.

Rams Head

2-4 Moss Street

A Magees beerhouse which closed in 1939.

Recreation Tavern

1 Hobson Street

A Tongs, later Walkers beerhouse which closed in 1959 as part of an agreement to transfer the licence of the Roebuck, Kay Street, to the new Prince Rupert, Holmeswood Road.

The Poplar Inn in 1952

Returned Sailor *See Gladstone Hotel*

Rifle Volunteer *See Volunteer*

Robin Hood

370 Halliwell Road

A beerhouse with its own brewery in the nineteenth century. It was acquired by Seeds Brewery of Radcliffe, who rebuilt the premises in 1898. Subsequently owned by Duttons, the Robin Hood was fully licensed in 1950 and later became a Whitbread pub.

(Old) Robin Hood

174-178 Lever Street

A Sharmans public house which closed in 1933 when the licence was transferred to the Nightingale Inn. (See Greengate Inn)

Robin Hood

4 Slater Lane

An Alexandra Brewery beerhouse, later owned by Magees. It became fully licensed in 1962 and closed in 1978.

Rock House Hotel

65-67 Duke Street

A beerhouse until 1882, when owner James Drennan acquired the full licence of the Shakespeare, a Bradshawgate pub which had closed a few years earlier, from the Corporation. Later owners have included Chadwick's Walmersley Brewery of Bury, Walker & Homfray of Salford and Wilsons. Today it is a Banks's Brewery pub.

Rope & Anchor

198-200 Kay Street

A Settles, later Duttons beerhouse which became fully licensed in 1962 and closed in 1971.

Rose & Crown

55 Cross Street

A beerhouse with its own brewery which was subsequently owned by Settles and then Duttons. It closed about 1960.

Queens Hotel, Darley Street

Rose Hill

122 Manchester Road

A fully licensed house, opened about 1830. In the first half of the twentieth century the Rose Hill was owned by the Lancashire & Yorkshire Railway Company. It later became a Magees and then a Greenall Whitley pub. In the 1980s it became a free house called Churchills.

Rothwell Street Tavern

34 Rothwell Street

A beerhouse with its own brewery, in the late nineteenth century owned by Thomas Howcroft, whose company later had the Spa Road brewery. Tetleys of Leeds were the owners when it got its full licence in 1961. The pub closed about 1970.

Roundcroft Tavern

50 James Street

In the late nineteenth century this was a beerhouse with its own brewery. Wilsons were the owners when it became fully licensed in 1962 and when it closed in 1965.

Royal George

59 Blackburn Road

A beerhouse, owned by Magees and then Sharmans, which closed in 1922.

Royal Hotel

53 Vernon Street

A fully licensed house which in the late nineteenth century was owned by the Gee family (Robert was the licensee of the Royal; John had the Railway on St Helens Road). Threlfalls of Salford were the next owners and the Royal subsequently became a Whitbread house. It is now owned by Avebury Taverns.

The Roundcroft Tavern in the 1960s

Royal Oak

73 Bury Old Road

A beerhouse with its own brewery in the nineteenth century. It was acquired by Messrs Watson, Woodhead & Wagstaffe, brewers of Salford, who merged with Walker & Homfrays in 1912. The Royal Oak closed in 1922.

Royal Oak

117 Kay Street

A beerhouse which belonged to the Alexandra Brewery and then Magees and closed in 1968.

Royal Tiger

4 Noble Street

A Sharmans beerhouse, closed in 1911.

The Old Robin Hood, Lever Street, in the 1920s

Rushton Arms

28 Wareing Street
A beerhouse owned by Swales Brewery of Hulme and then Hamers of Bromley Cross. It closed in 1913.

St James Hotel

1-3 Buxton Street
A beerhouse owned by Magees and then Swales of Hulme. It closed in the 1970s.

St John's Tavern

45 St John Street
A beerhouse which had its own brewery in the nineteenth century and was later owned by Magees. It closed in the 1960s.

Sally Up Steps *See Stanley Arms*

School Hill Hotel

6 School Hill
A beerhouse with its own brewery. It was owned by the licensee, Mrs Ellen Crompton, in the 1880s and later became a Settles house. Duttons were the owners when it became fully licensed in 1960 and the pub closed in the 1970s.

Sefton Arms

22 Brougham Street
An Alexandra Brewery beerhouse, later Magees, which closed in the 1970s.

Sir Sidney Smith in the 1920s

Shakespeare Tavern *See Lord Napier*

Shamrock Bar *See Railway Hotel*

Shamrock Inn

31 Soho Street
A beerhouse, owned in the 1880s by Mark O'Boyle, licensee of the Derby Arms on Derby Street. It was subsequently a Magees house and closed about 1905.

Sharman Arms *See Derby Hotel*

Sir Colin Campbell

166 Folds Road
In the 1880s this was owned by George Walker, proprietor of the Park View Brewery, Spa Road. James Jackson & Sons later owned the brewery and the beerhouse, which closed in 1913.

Sir Sidney Smith

131 Bridgeman Street
Opened 1808. A Sharmans pub which closed in 1934, when the licence was transferred to the Ninehouse Tavern.

Smoothing Iron *See Junction Inn*

Spinners Arms
Derby Street - see Stanley Arms

Spinners Arms

10-12 Liverpool Street
A beerhouse owned by the Alexandra Brewery and then Magees. It closed in 1915.

Spinners Arms

82-84 Lyon Street
A Sharmans, later Walkers beerhouse which closed about 1960.

Spinners Arms

20 Mill Street
A beerhouse owned by Wingfields, then the Manchester Brewery Company. The licence was refused in 1905.

Spinners Arms

89-91 Mill Hill Street
A Sharmans beerhouse which closed in 1933.

The Spinners Arms, Lyon Street, in the 1920s

Spinners Arms
Nelson St - see Nelson Arms

Spotted Cow *See Cattle Market*

Stags Head
196 St Helens Road
A fully licensed house which had its own brewery in the nineteenth century. It belonged to Tongs and then Walkers before becoming a Tetley pub.

Standard Arms
50-52 Hulme Street
A beerhouse owned by James Hall, proprietor of the Spread Eagle, Eagley, in the nineteenth century. It became a Magees house and closed in 1911.

Standard Hotel
19 Gray Street
A beerhouse owned by the Prince Arthur Brewery and then by Tongs. It closed in 1938.

Stanley Arms
99 Chorley Old Road
A Tongs, later Walkers and then Tetley house, renamed Sally Up Steps in the 1980s.

Stanley Arms
134 Derby Street
A beerhouse, originally known as the Spinners, which was owned by the Crown Brewing Company of Bury and then Duttons. It became fully licensed in 1961 and closed in 1973.

Stanley Arms
1 Egyptian Street
A beerhouse with its own brewery in the nineteenth century. It became a Sharmans and later a Walkers house and closed about 1960.

The Stork Tavern in the 1920s

Stork Tavern
548 Halliwell Road
Originally a Sharmans, later a Walkers beerhouse. It became fully licensed in 1962 and today is called the Fox & Stork.

Sunray Hotel
74 Mill Street
A beerhouse, originally called the Weavers Arms, which was owned by the Crown Brewing Company of Bury and closed in 1907.

Swiss Hotel
8-10 Southern Street
An Atkinsons and later Cornbrook pub which closed in the 1970s.

Tanners Arms
61-63 Lever Street
A beerhouse with its own brewery in the nineteenth century and originally called the Farmers Arms. Owners included Alfred Crowther of the Star Brewery, Bury, the Alexandra Brewery and Magees. It was fully licensed in

The Stanley Arms, Egyptian Street, in the 1920s

1962 and was a Greenalls house when it closed in 1986.

Tippings Arms

312 Blackburn Road
A fully licensed house, opened in the 1820s, which was later owned by Eden & Thwaites, bleachers, and then by Threlfalls Brewery of Salford. It became a Whitbread pub and today is called the Bedrock Cafe.

Tramways Hotel

307 Blackburn Road
In 1881 the licence of the Red Lion on Deansgate (see Part Three) was transferred to the new Tramways Hotel, which had been built on the site of an old beerhouse and butcher's shop. The hotel became a Magees pub and was later acquired by Greenalls.

Uncle Tom's Cabin

69 Egyptian Street
A beerhouse which in the 1880s was owned by George Walker, proprietor of the Park View Brewery, Spa Road. It was later owned by James Jackson & Sons and closed in 1911.

Uncle Tom's Cabin

270-272 Lever Street
A beerhouse which had its own brewery until the 1930s. It was subsequently owned by Hamers, then Duttons and became fully licensed in 1953. The pub is now called the New Cabin.

Union Arms

53 Bullock Street
A fully licensed house with its own brewery, opened in the 1820s. It was later owned by Tongs, Jackson's Spa Road Brewery, Shaws of Leigh and then Walkers. It closed in 1969.

Waggon & Horses, Manchester Road, in the 1920s

Union Arms

63-65 Deane Road
A Shaws beerhouse, closed in 1933.

Union Arms

56-58 Eskrick Street
A beerhouse owned by the Whitefield Brewery Company at the beginning of the twentieth century and then by J W Lees of Middleton Junction. Later owners were Hamers and then Duttons. A full licence was granted in 1960 and the pub closed in 1979.

Union Arms

53-55 Union Street
A beerhouse owned by Groves & Whitnall of Salford which closed in 1912.

Venture Street Tavern

See White House

Victoria

238 Bridgeman Street
A beerhouse with its own brewery in the nineteenth century. Later it was owned by the Alexandra Brewery, Magees and then Greenall Whitley. It closed in the 1990s.

Victoria Hotel

33 Lum Street
A beerhouse owned by Atkinsons and later the Cornbrook Brewery which closed in 1913.

Victoria British Queen

124 Blackburn Road
A former beerhouse owned by the Alexandra Brewery, then Magees and later Greenall Whitley.

Victory Hotel

151 Chorley Old Road
In the 1890s this pub was owned by John Haslam & Co Ltd of the Halliwell Cotton Works. It later became a Magees and then a Greenalls house.

Volunteer

151 Blackburn Road
A Sharmans beerhouse, earlier known as the Rifle Volunteer, which closed in 1934.

Waggon Hotel

4-6 Blackburn Road
A public house first recorded as the Waggon & Horses in 1803. It was a Magees pub when it closed about 1970.

Union Arms, Bullock Street, in the 1920s

Waggon & Horses
160 Manchester Road
A Sharmans, then Walkers beerhouse which became fully licensed in 1961.

Waggon & Horses
69 St Helens Road
A Magees beerhouse which closed in the 1970s.

Waterloo Hotel
306 Waterloo Street
A fully licensed house, opened in 1820 and owned by a Manchester spirit merchant, Henry Carswell, in the latter part of the nineteenth century. It became a Magees house and closed in the 1960s.

Waterloo Tavern
197-199 Folds Road
In the 1880s this was a beerhouse owned by George Walker, proprietor of the Park View Brewery, Spa Road. James Jackson & Sons were the next owners, then Shaws, followed by Walkers. A full licence was granted in 1961 and the pub closed in the 1970s.

Weavers Arms
8 Brunel Street
A Hamers, then Duttons beerhouse which became fully licensed in 1960. It was later a Whitbread pub and is now a free house.

Weavers Arms
88 Deane Road
A beerhouse owned by Atkinsons and later the Cornbrook Brewery. It became fully licensed in 1961 and closed a few years later.

Weavers Arms
Mill Street - see Sunray Hotel

The Windsor Castle in the 1920s

Welcome Inn
16 Victoria Street
An Alexandra Brewery, later Magees beerhouse which closed in the 1970s.

Wellington Hotel
51 Bury New Road
A fully licensed house once owned by the Crown Brewing Company, Bury, then Duttons and today Whitbread.

Wheatsheaf
76 Deane Road
A beerhouse which was owned in the 1880s by Mark O'Boyle, licensee of the Derby Arms on Derby Street. It was subsequently a Magees house and closed in the 1970s.

The Welcome Inn, Victoria Street

White Hart
157 Deane Road
This public house was first licensed in 1808 and still had its own brewery in the late nineteenth century. It became a Tongs, then Walkers and later a Tetleys house. The pub was rebuilt in the 1960s and in the 1980s was renamed Carringtons. It closed a few years later.

White House
213 Bridgeman Street
A beerhouse called the Venture Street Tavern until 1925. It was owned by Henry Heyes of the Fox Brewery (Fox & Goose beerhouse), Deansgate (see Part Three), in the 1870s, and later by the Grants Tower Brewery of Ewood Bridge. The White House closed in the 1970s.

Whitsters Arms *See Crofters Hotel*

Windmill Inn
60 Deane Road
A Sharmans, later Walkers beerhouse which became fully licensed in 1962 and closed in the 1970s.

Windsor Castle
37 Halliwell Road
Like the Windmill, this was a Sharmans, later Walkers beerhouse which became fully licensed in 1962 and closed in the 1970s.

Woodman Inn
1 Carlyle Street
A beerhouse which belonged to James Leach of the Albert Brewery, then Cunninghams of Warrington and Tetleys of Leeds. It became fully licensed in 1961 and closed about 1970.

York Street Tavern
48 York Street
A beerhouse which was owned by the Alexandra Brewery and then Magees. It closed in the 1960s.

Part Three

BOLTON PUBS 1800-1900

This list of licensed houses which had closed by the end of the nineteenth century is based on alehouse records in the Lancashire County Record Office, Bolton's licensing records and reports of licensing meetings, Bolton directories and a list of Great and Little Bolton public houses and beerhouses which was compiled for the Bolton Corporation Nuisance Committee on 6th April 1849.

Beerhouses - permitted to sell beer, or beer and wine, but not spirits - began to open following the 1830 Licensing Act and the issuing of beer licences was not brought under strict control until the late 1860s. By the time the 1849 list was compiled there were already more beerhouses in Bolton than there were public houses. The list contains the names of seventy-two in Great Bolton and thirty-one in Little Bolton, and there were another fifty in Great Bolton and thirty-one in Little Bolton without names or signs.

Most of the public houses listed here were pulled down for town centre improvements and industrial development between the 1860s and the 1890s. When they closed, their full licences were usually transferred to new buildings or to already existing beerhouses in other parts of the town. As for the beerhouses, the sites of many can be identified, but some of those which are named on the 1849 list seem to have existed for only a few years and their exact locations may never be known!

Albion Hotel

24 Bridgeman Street
Closed in 1899, when the property was owned by the Lancashire & Yorkshire Railway Company.

Albion Inn

Cricket Street
A beerhouse occupied by William Almond in 1869, when the licence was refused.

Anchor *See Rope & Anchor*

Ancient Shepherd

Newport Street
A beerhouse occupied by Andrew Rock in 1849 and not to be confused with the Ancient Shepherd of recent memory on Bold Street, which in 1849 was called the Oddfellows Arms. This Ancient Shepherd seems to have been on the west side of Newport Street and may have been renamed the Star Vaults.

Angel & Woolpack

Deansgate
An old alehouse, listed in licensing records simply as the Woolpack from the 1770s until about 1820. It stood on the opposite corner of Mealhouse Lane to the Old Woolpack (see Part One) and when it closed in 1874 the licence was transferred to the Vulcan Inn on Great Moor Street.

Anglers Home

Queen Street
A Magees beerhouse, formerly known as the Queen Street Tavern. The licence was surrendered in 1898.

Antelopes Head

Churchgate
An alehouse listed in licensing records from the 1790s. It stood on the north side of Churchgate, between the Golden Lion and the Boars Head, and when it closed in 1880 the full licence was transferred to the Portland Hotel on Portland Street.

Bank Inn

Bank Street
A public house which opened in 1808. It was on the west side of the street, near the bridge over the Croal, and was pulled down in 1872 for the building of the Unitarian Schools.

GRAPES HOTEL,
BOLTON.
SIMPSON & Co.'s
CELEBRATED
OLD ALES,
Tenpenny, Fourteenpenny, AND Eighteenpenny.
OLD WINES & SPIRITS
Of the Choicest Description.
All Spirits thoroughly Matured.
LONDON, Manchester, Yorkshire, Edinburgh, and all the Local Newspapers taken daily, also the Illustrated and Comic Papers.
Thos. Simpson & Co.,
Wine & Spirit Merchants,
Town Hall Square,
BOLTON.

1894 advertisement

The Portland Hotel in the 1920s. The licence from the Antelopes Head on Churchgate was transferred here in 1880

Barley Mow
Higher Bridge Street
A Tongs beerhouse which closed in 1875. It was on the left hand side, just past Prince Street.

Barrack Tavern
See Wellington Inn

Bee Hive
Folds Road
A beerhouse occupied by James Battersby in 1869, when the licence was refused. It was listed at 9&11 Folds Road and was later used as shop premises.

Bird i'th'Hand
Bank Street
An old public house which was in existence in the 1770s. It stood across from the Unitarian Chapel and lost its licence in 1870. The building was being used as a lodging house by 1876.

Black Boy
Moor Lane
A beerhouse kept by Simon Hilton in 1849. It was located at the southern end of Moor Lane and was closed in 1869.

Black Bull *See Bulls Head*

Black Cow
Moor Lane
A beerhouse kept by Joseph Horrock in 1849.

Blue Bell
Spring Gardens
A beerhouse kept by Thomas Foster in 1849. It appears to have opened in the 1830s and was numbered 63 Spring Gardens in 1853.

LORD CLYDE BREWERY,
107 & 109, Folds Road, and 1, Phœnix Street,
LITTLE BOLTON.

THOMAS HOLDEN, Proprietor,
BREWER.

LORD CLYDE INN,
FOLDS ROAD.
This Inn is Noted for its MILD and BITTER ALES.
LONDON AND DUBLIN STOUT.
Retailer of FOREIGN WINES of the best quality.
FAMILIES SUPPLIED AT WHOLESALE PRICES.
THE MILL HILL CRICKET CLUB HELD AT THIS HOUSE.

1880 advertisement

Bowling Green *See Shakespeare*

Brinks Brow Tavern
Chorley Street
A beerhouse kept by Robert Crawford in 1849.

British Oak
Deansgate
A beerhouse which was occupied by Benjamin Law in 1869, when the licence was refused. The building was at number 117 Deansgate, between Spring Gardens and Back Spring Gardens. Mr Law was listed there as a fruiterer in 1870 and by 1876 it was a butcher's shop. The firm of Hart's, pork butchers, was still there in the 1960s.

Buffalo Arms
Kay Street
A beerhouse occupied by John Wood when the licence was refused in 1869.

Bulls Head
Bradshawgate
An eighteenth century alehouse later known as the Black Bull. It stood on the corner of Wood Street and was demolished in 1894 for the District Bank.

Bury Street Tavern
Bury Street
A beerhouse whose licence was refused in 1869 because the premises were in poor condition and very dirty.

Bus Drivers Inn
Bradshawgate
A beerhouse which stood on the south corner of Silverwell Lane. The licence was refused in 1883.

Canary Tavern
Charles Street
A beerhouse occupied by John Metcalfe in 1849. It had closed by 1870.

Carters Arms
Chorley Street
A beerhouse occupied by John Morris when the licence was refused in 1869.

Chelsea Pensioner
Deansgate
A beerhouse occupied by John Walsh in 1849. It was on White Lion Brow and may have been an earlier name for the Gipsy's Tent (see Part One).

The Windmill Inn, Deane Road, in the 1920s

1880 advertisement

Church Inn

Waterloo Street

A beerhouse which closed in 1884. It was on the south side of the street and numbered 235 in 1876.

Cloggers Arms

Deansgate

A beerhouse occupied by Henry Jones in 1849.

Cloggers Arms

Deansgate

A beerhouse occupied by Robert Kellett in 1849. In 1861 a Robert Kellett is listed at 118 Deansgate, which was the Bee Hive (see Part One) and may have been the same place.

Coachmakers Arms

Bradshawgate

A beerhouse which closed in 1884 and was pulled down for Corporation improvements. It was numbered 78 Bradshawgate and stood near the Balmoral.

Cock

Churchgate

Located on the north side of Churchgate, between the Golden Lion and the Boars Head. It is listed in licensing records from the 1770s until the 1830s.

Cotton Tree

Moor Lane

A beerhouse occupied by Thomas Holt in 1849. It was at the south end of Moor Lane and closed in 1869.

Crooked Billet

Churchgate

A beerhouse occupied by James Sharples in 1849. The licence was refused in 1869 and thereafter Mr Sharples ran the establishment as an eating house.

Cross Axes

Woods Court

An old alehouse which is listed in licensing records from the 1770s, both as the Cross Axes and the Crown & Anchor. It closed in 1879, when the licence was transferred to the Market Hotel, Ashburner Street. Woods Court was on the north side of Deansgate, between Bridge Street and Crown Street.

Cross Keys

Churchgate

An old licensed house which dated from the eighteenth century and stood near the Parish Church. It closed in the 1850s or early 1860s.

Crown

Deansgate

An old alehouse which was located in an entry opposite the end of Crown Street. It is listed in licensing records from the 1770s and closed in 1872.

Crown & Anchor *See Cross Axes*

Dog *See Talbot*

Druids Arms

Bradshawgate

A beerhouse occupied by Josiah Hurst in 1849. It was possibly part of a row of buildings on the west side of the street, near the Balmoral, which were pulled down about 1875.

Duke of York *See Lamb Inn*

Farmers Arms

Bradshawgate

A beerhouse occupied by James Waring in 1849.

Farmers Arms

Deane Road

A beerhouse, numbered 190-192 Pikes Lane (later Deane Road), which lost its licence in 1869. It was owned by William Tong of the nearby Tongs Brewery, who arranged for the transfer of the Rifle Volunteer, Bridgeman

The Rainforth Hotel, School Hill, in the 1920s

Street, beerhouse licence to the premises in 1872. It became an off-licence and closed about four years later.

Flash Tavern

Derby Street

A beerhouse occupied by John Morris in 1849.

Fleece Tavern

Bridge Street

A beerhouse occupied by John Dewhurst in 1849.

Foresters Arms

Lum Street

A beerhouse which was occupied by William Holden when the licence was refused in 1869.

Fox & Goose

Deansgate

A beerhouse which stood on the north side of Deansgate. The licence was refused in 1897 and the building was demolished for the building of the Fire Station.

Friendship Arms

Spring Gardens

A beerhouse occupied by Richard Warburton when the licence was refused in 1869.

General Sir Robert Sale

Crook Street

A beerhouse which in the 1840s and 1850s was listed on Crook Street. The building appears to have been pulled down when the railway goods yard was enlarged.

RED LION HOTEL,

50, CROOK ST., BOLTON.

THOMAS BRADY, PROPRIETOR.

Having succeeded to the Agency of the celebrated WINES of VALLADOLID, SPAIN, as sold by the late REV. CANON CARTER, I have the pleasure to inform you that I shall always keep in stock a Choice Selection of the favourite Brands, the prices of which you will find below.

I remain, yours respectfully, THOMAS BRADY.

A Dry White	at 24/-	per Doz., or	£12	per qr. Cask of 27 Galls.
B Rich „	„ 25/-	„ „	£12 12/-	„ „ „
RR „ Red	„ 25/-	„ „	£12 12/-	„ „ „
Vino Puro Light White	„ 15/-	„ „	£7 5/-	„ „ „
Castilian „ Red	„ 17/6	„ „	£8 10/-	„ „ „
Golden Sherry, very fine	„ 28/-	„ „	£14 12/-	„ „ „

Spirits and other Wines in great variety. Single Bottles supplied.

This Hotel is 3 minutes walk from the L. & N. W. Station, and 5 minutes walk from the L. & Y. Station.

1880 advertisement

General Sir Robert Sale

Newport Street

This beerhouse is recorded on the east side of Newport Street (No.97) in the 1860s and 1870s, so it may have been a replacement for the Crook Street beerhouse of the same name. The building was pulled down when the Lancashire & Yorkshire Railway built the Bolton Loop line and Newport Street bridge was enlarged.

Borough Arms, Higher Bridge Street, in the 1920s

Globe

Bridgeman Street

A beerhouse which was closed in 1869, for a number of reasons. The licensee allowed gambling on the premises, the clientele included prostitutes and there was a 'low singing room and dancing class' frequented by thieves and loose characters. There was also a minor objection on public health grounds because he kept pigs in the backyard.

Golden Lion

See White Bear

Good Samaritan

Kay Street

A beerhouse occupied by Thomas Knowles in 1849.

Greyhound

Bullock Street

A beerhouse occupied by John Hamer in 1849.

Grey Man

Old Hall Street

A beerhouse occupied by James Owen in 1849. It was probably on what became Old Hall Street South.

Hand & Shuttle

Fletcher Street

A beerhouse occupied by William Wood in 1849.

Happy as a King *See Park Inn*

Hare and Hounds

Derby Street

A beerhouse occupied by Jonathan Shaw when the licence was refused in 1869. It was possibly at 164 Derby Street, which was being used as a greengrocer's shop by 1870.

Hatters Arms

Bradshawgate

A beerhouse occupied by James Johnson in 1849.

(Old) Hen & Chickens

Deansgate

Located between the Blue Boar and the Kings Arms and in existence by the 1770s. It closed in 1888, when the licence was transferred to the Railway Shipping Inn (Brunswick Hotel) on Crook Street (see Part One).

Hope & Anchor

Churchgate(?)

This pub appears in licensing records from the 1770s until 1814. For many years it was kept by John Hardcastle, and this name also appears next to the Boars Head, Churchgate.

Horse & Groom

Bradshawgate

One of several old buildings between Great Moor Street and Nelson Square which were pulled down in the 1870s. The Horse & Groom is listed in licensing records from the 1770s and in 1875 the licence was transferred to the Duke of Clarence on Bath Street.

Horse & Jockey

Bradshawgate

A fully licensed house which appears to have opened in the 1790s. It stood on or near the site of the Balmoral Hotel and closed in 1875, when the licence was transferred to the Derby Arms on Derby Street (see Part Two).

John o'Gaunt

Chorley Street

A beerhouse kept by John Johnson in 1849. It possibly became the Derby Hotel (see Part One).

Joiners Arms

Mill Street

A beerhouse occupied by John Kay in 1849.

Jolly Carter

Bradshawgate

A beerhouse which was occupied by Robert Davis when the licence was refused in 1869.

Jolly Drummer

Green Street, Great Bolton

A beerhouse occupied by Susannah Ainscow in 1849.

Jolly Huxter

Cannon Street

A beerhouse occupied by James Whittle in 1849.

Jolly Sailor

Kay Street

A beerhouse occupied by Richard Cashmore in 1849.

Jolly Sportsman

Mill Hill Street

A beerhouse occupied by James Entwistle in 1849.

Jolly Sportsman

Cromwell Street - see Museum

Town Hall Hotel,

OLD HALL STREET SOUTH,

BOLTON.

THOMAS SETTLE, Proprietor.

This Hotel is centrally situated between the Town Hall, and the Wholesale Market, and about three minutes walk from the L. & N. W. Ry., and five minutes walk from the L. & Y. Ry. Stations, and Threatre Royal.

First class Wines, Ales and Porter Bottled or on Draught, Cigars, &c.

CLUBS HELD HERE.

The National Independent Order of Oddfellows' Bolton District—
"The Conquering Hero Lodge," No. 458, BOLTON.

GOOD STABLING.

1885 advertisement

The Recreation Tavern, Hobson Street, in the 1920s

Lamb Inn

Spring Gardens

This stood on the west side of Spring Gardens and was first licensed in 1817 as the Duke of York. It closed in 1899 and the site is now covered by the Magistrates' Courts.

Lamb Inn

Union Street

A beerhouse occupied by Thomas Johnson in 1849.

Little John

Ashburner Street

A beerhouse occupied by James Nuttall in 1849.

Lord Collingwood

Deansgate

A fully licensed house which opened in 1806 and closed in 1894, when it was a Magees house. It was on the north side of Deansgate, opposite Spring Gardens. The licence was transferred to the Oddfellows on St Helens Road.

Masons Arms

Fletcher Street

A beerhouse occupied by Stephen Winstanley in 1849.

Masons Arms

Location unknown

A public house listed in licensing records from 1808 to 1817.

Mechanics Arms

Kay Street

A beerhouse kept by Abraham Clegg in 1849. This may have become the Buck & Vine (see Part Two).

Golden Lion Hotel,

13, CHURCHGATE, BOLTON.

Mrs. Elizabeth Hamer,

PROPRIETORESS.

This old established Inn is near the spot where James, the 7th Earl of Derby was executed on October 15th, 1651, and is opposite the Theatre Royal and Museum Music Hall, and within easy distance from the Town Hall and the L. & N. W. Ry. and L. & Y. Ry. Stations.

Wines and Spirits, Ale and Porter,

Bottled or Draught of the best quality. Cigars of the Finest Brands.

Clubs held here:—"The Ancient Order of Druids;" "Sweet Green Burial Club."

Concert Room opened every Monday and Saturday.

1885 advertisement

Milk Street Tavern

Milk Street

A beerhouse, earlier known as the Old Ivy House. The licence was refused in 1894 because it was a 'disorderly house'.

Millstone

Deansgate

Not to be confused with the Old Millstone, the predecessor of the Millstone in Crown Street (see Part One), this inn was opposite, on the south side of Deansgate and at the end of Millstone Entry. When it closed in 1874 the licence was transferred to the Cricketers Arms on Hibbert Street (see Part Two).

Minders Arms

Bury Old Road

A beerhouse listed at 93 Bury Old Road and occupied by William Disley in 1869, when the licence was refused. In 1876 John Disley, brewer, is listed at the same address. The name Minders Arms reappears in directories in the 1890s, but the premises were being used as an off-licence in the 1920s and 1930s.

Morning Star

Moor Lane

A beerhouse which was owned by George Walker of the Spa Road Brewery when magistrates refused to renew the licence in 1891 because of the tenant's bad character. There was an appeal against the decision, but this was dismissed at the Quarter Sessions. The Morning Star stood at the Deane Road end of Moor Lane, on the north side.

Moulders Arms

Garside Street

A beerhouse occupied by Simon Hilton in 1849. The licence was refused in 1869.

Museum

Cromwell Street

A beerhouse which was located at the bottom of Gas Street and was demolished in 1883. It was also known as the Sportsman or the Jolly Sportsman.

The White Hart, Deane Road, in the 1920s

THE OLD WOOLPACK,

DEANSGATE, Corner of Mealhouse-lane.

THOMAS C. HIGSON, PROPRIETOR.

THIS Hotel is centrally situated, being within easy distance of the Market Hall, Theatre Royal, and L. & N. W. and L. & Y. Railway Stations. EVERY ACCOMODATION FOR VISITORS.

First-class Wines and Spirits.

MILD & BITTER ALES & STOUT.

CIGARS OF THE FINEST BRANDS.

1885 advertisement

Music Tavern

Gaskell's Court, off Churchgate

According to a report of the 1869 licensing sessions, this tavern was well known for more than just its music. The police stated that it was a notorious house and up to four 'loose girls' lived there. The licence was refused.

Nelson Arms

58 Nelson St

A beerhouse which seems to have closed in the 1880s or early 1890s. It was probably pulled down to make room for new buildings at Walkers Tannery and the name was transferred to the Spinners Arms at 11 Nelson Street (see Part Two).

New Inn

St Georges Road

A beerhouse whose licence was refused in 1869 because it was a 'resort and residence of prostitutes and other bad characters'. The building was probably at number 91, between Duke Street and Noel Street, and later became a furniture shop.

New Market Tavern

Bullock Street

A beerhouse occupied by Jane Lee in 1849.

New Market Tavern

Howell Croft

A beerhouse occupied by Robert Grime when the licence was refused in 1869.

Oak

Bury Old Road

A beerhouse occupied by Thomas Brooks and listed at 69 Bury Old Road in 1869, when the licence was refused.

Oddfellows Arms

Dawes Street

A beerhouse which was kept by John Barns in 1849. It probably closed in the 1860s.

Old House at Home

Old Acres

Old Acres was the old name for the end of Great Moor Street between Bradshawgate and Mawdsley Street. When the street was widened in 1875, this beerhouse was one of the casualties.

The Waterloo Tavern, Folds Road, in the 1920s

Old Horse Shoe

Location unknown

Listed in licensing records for 1804-1806 only

Old Ivy House *See Milk Street Tavern*

One Horse Shoe

New Market Place

Listed in the licensing records from the late eighteenth century until the 1860s. New Market Place became Town Hall Square and later Victoria Square. The One Horse Shoe was probably one of the properties demolished to make room for the building of the Town Hall.

Papermakers Arms

Bridgeman Place

A beerhouse occupied by Robert Lever in 1869, when the licence was refused. Mr Lever is last listed in the 1870 directory, when the address was 73 Bridgeman Place.

Park Inn

Spa Lane (later Spa Road)

A beerhouse numbered 39 Spa Lane and occupied by Thomas Rothwell when the licence was refused in 1869. It was better known as the Happy as a King.

Pen Street Arms

Pen Street

A beerhouse occupied by Robert Wood in 1869, when the licence appears to have been refused.

Plasterers Arms

Union Street

A beerhouse occupied by James Grime in 1849.

Pleasant View

Vernon Street

A beerhouse which was occupied by

Thomas Slater when the licence was refused in 1869.

Prince of Wales

Moncrieffe Street

A beerhouse occupied by Thomas Williams when the licence was refused in 1869. The premises, at 111 Moncrieffe Street, were in use as a grocery and draper's shop by 1876.

Queen Elizabeth

Blackhorse Street

This was a fully licensed house which from the 1840s until about 1870 stood on the part of Blackhorse Street between Great Moor Street and Crook Street. It was pulled down along with adjoining property so that a new Great Moor Street Station could be built. In 1874 the licence was transferred to the refreshment rooms at the new station, but this didn't last. After just six years the refreshment room licence was refused and railway travellers had to make do with cups of tea.

Queen Elizabeth

Bradshawgate

A fully licensed house, dating from 1800 or earlier, which stood on the west side of Bradshawgate, between Great Moor Street and Bollings Yard and next door to the Bowling Green Inn (later the Shakespeare). It was also known as the Queens Head and closed in the early 1840s. The licence was probably transferred to the Queen Elizabeth on Blackhorse Street.

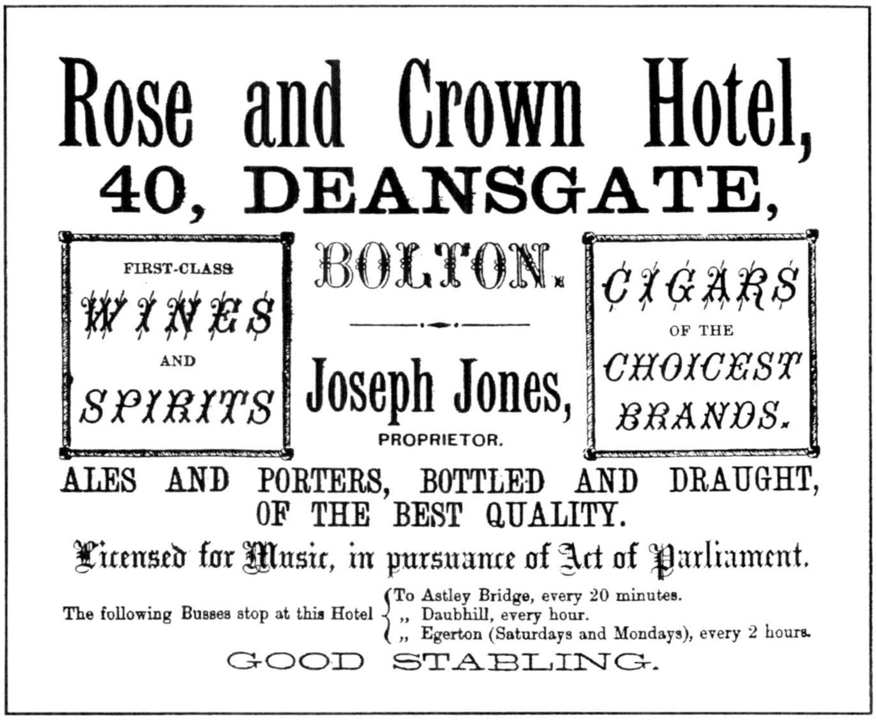

1880 advertisement

Queens Head

See Queen Elizabeth, Bradshawgate

Queen Street Tavern

See Anglers Home

The Gilnow Arms, Deane Road, in the 1920s

Railway Bridge Inn

Dawes Street

A beerhouse occupied by Leonard Fielden when the licence was refused in 1869.

Railway Tavern

Bradshawgate

A beerhouse occupied by Edmund Harwood in 1849.

Railway Tavern

Great Moor Street

A beerhouse which stood across from the George Hotel and was demolished in the early 1870s for the rebuilding of Great Moor Street Station.

Rainbow Tavern

Kay Street

A beerhouse occupied by William Hartley in 1849.

Red House

Spring Gardens

A beerhouse occupied by Elizabeth Cooper when the licence was refused in 1869. It was numbered 70 Spring Gardens in 1864.

Red Lion

Deansgate

Located between the Joiners Arms and the Old Woolpack on the corner of Mealhouse Lane (see Part One). The Red Lion was in existence in the 1770s and it closed in 1881 when the licence was transferred to the Tramways Hotel on Blackburn Road (see Part Two).

Rifle Volunteer

Bow Street

A beerhouse which closed in 1869 when the licensee was Nancy Stott.

Rifle Volunteer

Bridgeman Street
A beerhouse which closed in 1872 when the licence was transferred to the Farmers Arms on Pikes Lane (Deane Road).

Ring o'Bells

Location unknown
An alehouse which appears in licensing records between 1801 and 1806.

Ring o'Bells

Kay Street
A beerhouse occupied by Thomas Duggleby in 1849.

Rising Sun

Kay Street
A beerhouse occupied by Thomas Warburton in 1849. The licence was refused in 1869.

Rope & Anchor

Deansgate
A public house, listed simply as the Anchor in eighteenth century licensing records. It stood on the north side of Deansgate, between Market Street and Bridge Street, and when it closed in 1899 the licence was transferred to the Halliwell Lodge Hotel on Mornington Road (see Part Two).

Rose & Crown

Deansgate
This public house appears in the 1778 licensing records and it stood on the other side of Deansgate from the Lower Nags Head. It closed in 1884, when the licence was transferred to the Railway Hotel, 2 St Helens Road (see Part Two).

Bull and Wharf Hotel,

CHURCH WHARF, BOLTON.

THOMAS SHERRINGTON, Proprietor.

This old-established Hotel is about one minute's walk from the Parish Church, and is conveniently situated on the Bury Turnpike Road.

WINES & SPIRITS OF THE FIRST QUALITY.

The FINEST ALES and PORTERS, Bottled or Draught.

Cigars of the Choicest Brands. Good Stabling.

1880 advertisement

Rose & Crown

Kay Street
A beerhouse occupied by John Hart which lost its licence in 1869. The building, at 23 Kay Street, was subsequently used by a soft drinks manufacturer.

Royal Hotel

Derby Street
A beerhouse occupied by Abraham Ogden in 1869 when the licence was refused. In 1870 Abraham Ogden is listed as a coal dealer at 189 Derby Street, which may have been the same place. Six years later the building, between Hammond Street and Cricket Street, was being used as a tripe shop.

Royal Marine Tavern

Bridgeman Street
A beerhouse occupied by Edward Manchester Hall in 1849. It is likely that this was an earlier name for the Lord Napier (see Part Two).

Royal Oak

Bolton Street
A beerhouse occupied by William

The Nelson Hotel, Chorley Old Road, in the 1920s

Eckersley which is mentioned in a licensing report of 1869.

Royal Oak

Churchgate

This old pub was in existence in the 1770s and it closed about 1850. Location uncertain, but not the same building as the later Royal Oak beerhouse on Paley Street (see Prince of Wales in Part One).

Royal Order of Druids

York Street

A beerhouse kept by Mary Ann Crompton in 1849. This may have been an earlier name for the York Street Tavern (see Part Two).

Royal Tiger

Duncan Street

A beerhouse occupied by James Greenhalgh in 1849.

Seven Stars

Bank Street

An old public house dating from the 1770s or before. It stood on the west side of Bank Street, between the Unitarian Chapel and the Bank Inn. The Seven Stars closed in the 1860s or 1870s and the Unitarian Schools were built on the site of both pubs.

Shakespeare Inn

Bradshawgate

The Shakespeare stood on the west side of Bradshawgate, between Great Moor Street and Bollings Yard. Before the 1840s the pub here was called the Bowling Green and this is listed in licensing records back to the 1770s. The Shakespeare closed in the 1870s and the building was pulled down for Corporation improvements. In 1882 the full licence was transferred to the Rock House Hotel on Duke Street (see Part Two).

FLAG INN,

GREAT MOOR STREET, BOLTON.

Proprietress:

MRS. ELLEN HARRISON, BREWER.

This old-established Inn is centrally situated, being near the L. & N. W. Railway Station, the Wholesale Market, the Temple Opera House, and about two minutes walk from the L. & Y. Railway Station.

WINES & SPIRITS OF THE FIRST QUALITY.

Ale and Porter, Bottled or on Draught.

CIGARS of the Finest Brands. *Families supplied.* *Good Stabling.*

1880 advertisement

The Union Arms, Deane Road, in the 1920s

Sir Home Popham

Location unknown

A public house kept by Edward Ridgeway which appears in the licensing records for 1806 only. Sir Home Popham was an admiral of the time.

Sizers Arms

Spa Lane (later Spa Road)

A beerhouse, occupied by David Stansfield, which appears in the 1849 list.

Smith Street Tavern

Smith Street

A beerhouse listed in 1869, when it was occupied by Peter Morris.

Spinners Arms

Spa Lane (later Spa Road)

A beerhouse occupied by John Roscoe when the licence was refused in 1869.

Sportsman *See Museum*

Squirrel Tavern

White Lion Brow

A beerhouse occupied by Richard Parker in 1849. It was listed at No.28 White Lion Brow in 1864 and had closed by the 1870s.

Standard Hotel

Haydock Street

A beerhouse which is mentioned in a report of the 1869 licensing meeting. The tenant was Benjamin Atkinson.

Star Vaults

Newport Street

A beerhouse on the corner of Newport Street and Markland Street, across from where Ault's shop is today. The licence was refused in 1884 because the premises were 'not structurally adapted for business'.

Stone Jug

Kay Street

A beerhouse occupied by John Reynolds when the licence was refused in 1869. By the 1890s the building, which was at number 33 Kay Street and on the corner of St Georges Street, was being used as a lodging house.

Strangers Home

Dawes Street

A beerhouse which lost its licence in 1872 because the premises were 'unsuitable'.

Sun Inn

Bradshawgate

Not to be confused with the fully licensed Sun Inn on Bradshawgate (see Part One), this was a beerhouse which was occupied by John Lomax in 1849.

Tailors Goose

Spring Gardens

A beerhouse occupied by Jane Myers in 1849.

ROBIN HOOD INN,

40, ASHBURNER STREET, BOLTON.

ELLEN ASHTON, PROPRIETRESS,

BREWER.

This Inn is about two minutes walk from the Station, near the Wholesale Market; therefore it is in all respects the most convenient for market people and other travellers.

FIRST-CLASS WINES AND SPIRITS.

MILD and BITTER ALES, Bottled and Draught.

CIGARS of the Finest Brands. Good Stabling.

1880 advertisement

Talbot

Brown Street

An old alehouse dating from the 1770s or earlier. The licence was surrendered in 1879 so that a new licence could be granted to the Railway Hotel on Trinity Street.

Three Arrows

Old Hall Street

A public house which opened in 1817 and was closed and demolished in 1873, when the licence was transferred to the Park Hotel on Bridgeman Street (see Part Two).

The Rock House on Duke Street in 1952. It became fully licensed in 1882 following the closure of the Shakespeare Inn on Bradshawgate

Three Crowns

Deansgate

Opened in the late eighteenth century, the Three Crowns was on the other side of Deansgate from the Old Three Crowns and faced the top of Bridge Street. It was pulled down for Corporation improvements and in 1876 the licence was transferred to the new Balmoral Hotel.

Town Hall Hotel

All Saints Street

A fully licensed house, opened in the 1840s and closed by the 1870s.

Travellers Rest

Bark Street

A beerhouse occupied by Thomas Thornley when the licence was refused in 1869. The premises, number 164 Bark Street, eventually became a grocer's shop.

Travellers Rest

Newport Street

A beerhouse which closed about 1870. The three-storey building can still be seen, adjoining Ault's shop.

Turks Head

Bridge Street

A beerhouse demolished in 1882 for street improvements. It stood on the west side of the street, across from the end of Bow Street.

Unicorn

Deansgate

A beerhouse occupied by Timothy Kavanagh in 1849. The licence was refused in 1869.

Volunteer

Location unknown

A public house, kept by James Warr, which appears in licensing records for a few years until 1803.

Volunteer Canteen

Fletcher Street

Appears in a list of applicants for beerhouse certificates in 1869. The licensee was George Leach and the premises were presumably part of the barracks on Fletcher Street.

Warpers Arms

Watt Street

A beerhouse occupied by Thomas Daykin when the licence was refused in 1870. The premises were numbered 1 & 3 Watt Street and were subsequently used as a provision shop.

Weavers Arms

Ship Gates

A beerhouse listed in 1849 and gone by the 1870s. The building may have become a lodging house.

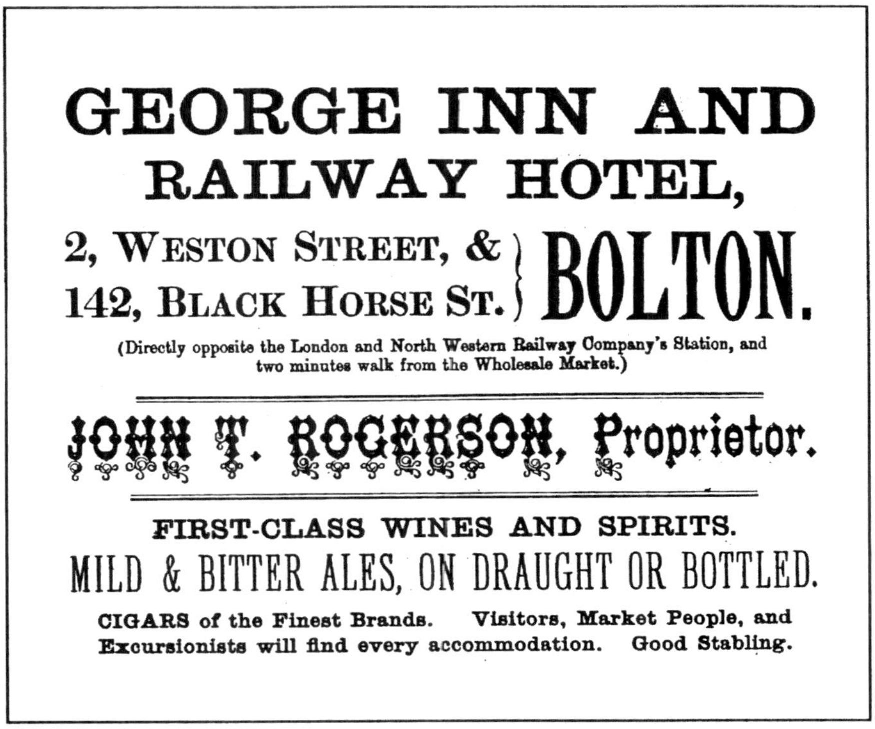

1880 advertisement

Welcome Traveller

Deansgate

A beerhouse listed in 1869 as occupied by Thomas Kellett. It may have been at number 118, which became the Bee Hive (see Part One).

Wellington Inn

Garside Street

In the 1830s this was a beerhouse, then by 1843 it was listed as the Barrack Tavern public house. The name was changed to the Wellington Inn and Threlfalls Brewery were the owners in 1875 when the pub closed and was pulled down. The licence was transferred to the Queen Elizabeth on Fletcher Street (see Part Two).

Wharf Inn

Church Wharf

A beerhouse occupied by Edward Birch in 1869, when the licence was refused.

White Bear

Deansgate

Listed in the records from the 1770s until 1801, when it became the Golden Lion. It was the White Bear again in the 1860s. The pub stood in a court on south side of Deansgate, near the Bradshawgate corner, and the licence was transferred to the Bradford Hotel, Bradford Street (see Part Two), in 1880.

White Dog

Bank Street

A beerhouse, located at 6&8 Bank Street, which the police claimed was being used as a brothel in 1869. The licensee said that the two girls who were living there were employed as 'servants' and since the girls were changed regularly, the police were unable to prove their case. The magistrates decided to close the beerhouse anyway.

White Dog

Grime Street (later St Edmund Street)

A beerhouse kept by Thomas Lawson in 1849. It had closed by the 1860s.

Wood Cutter

Crook Street

A beerhouse occupied by Nancy Bates in 1849.

Woolpack

See Angel & Woolpack

The Caledonian Inn, Lyon Street, in the 1920s

Part Four

THE BREWERIES

Bank Top Brewery

Twenty-five years after the closure of Magee Marshall's Crown Brewery, John Feeney, a former lorry driver, launched the Bank Top Brewery in October 1995. Based in an industrial unit off Vernon Street, he now brews 720 gallons a week and supplies over forty pubs covering an extensive area. His brews, which vary between 3.8% and 5%, have included Samuel Crompton's Ale, Fred's Cap, Satanic Mills 2 - Judgement Day, Gold Digger, Brydge Bitter, Cliffhanger, Smokestack Lightnin' and Santa's Claus. At the time of writing he is working his way through the names of twelve of the most popular Knights of the Round Table. In 1999 John obtained planning permission to remove the brewery to a Grade Two listed building in Bank Top and, after alterations, he hopes to be established there in the near future.

The old brewing companies

Since the 1890s Bolton has been home to several major breweries and another, Hamers, was just over the border at Bromley Cross. Dates of company registration and cessation of the following local breweries and brewers are as detailed in the all-embracing directory of British brewery companies, 'Where Have All The Breweries Gone?' by Norman Barber (1980). In one or two instances I have made minor additions and also collated individual items of information under one heading.

John Atkinson & Co Ltd

Commission Street Brewery

William Atkinson, wholesale brewer, had premises on Commission Street in the 1870s and by 1881 the business had expanded and John Atkinson was in charge. The company was taken over by Boardman's United Breweries Ltd of Cheetham, Manchester, in 1895. Three years later all this company's Lancashire pubs were acquired by the Cornbrook Brewery. Bass Charrington took over in 1961.

Bolton & District Clubs Brewery

See Bolton Free Brewery Co Ltd.

Bolton Free Brewery Co Ltd

Model Brewery, Spa Road

Registered in 1928 to acquire the bottling business carried on by Fred Leigh & Co. Successors to James Jackson & Sons Ltd in the use of the Model Brewery. Name changed to Bolton and District Clubs Brewery Co Ltd in 1929. Succeeded by Howcroft's in 1937.

J Halliwell & Son

Alexandra Brewery, Mount Street

Founded in 1856 by J Halliwell. Ceased trading in 1910 when acquired by Magee Marshall & Co Ltd.

Magee Marshall's brewery offices on Cricket Street in the 1970s

Howcroft's Brewery Ltd

Model Brewery, Spa Road

Much earlier, under Walker's Bolton Brewery Co Ltd and the Spa Wells Brewery Co Ltd, this was the Park View Brewery (erected 1874). Howcroft's originated at 32 Rothwell Street and moved to the Model Brewery in 1937 in succession to the Bolton & District Clubs Brewery Ltd. Merged with B Cunningham Ltd of Warrington in 1969 and the brewery ceased production later that year.

James Jackson & Sons Ltd

Model Brewery, Spa Road

Acquired the Model Brewery from the Spa Wells Brewery Co Ltd in 1904 and registered as a private company in 1913. Taken over by George Shaw & Co Ltd of Leigh in 1927. Shaw's were taken over by Walker Cain Ltd of Warrington in 1931 and the latter joined with Joshua Tetley & Sons Ltd in 1961 to form Tetley Walker Ltd.

Leach's Brewery Ltd

Albert Brewery, Hammond Street, Bantry Street and Albert Inn, 181-183 Derby Street

The business was founded at the Albert Inn in the 1850s by James Leach. Limited company registered 1905. Brewing ceased after 1937.

Magee Marshall & Co Ltd

Crown Brewery, Cricket Street, off Derby Street

Founded by David Magee of the Crown Hotel, 213 Derby Street, in the 1860s. Earlier, Daniel Magee was a beerhousekeeper at the Good Samaritan, 73 Derby Street. The firm acquired Daniel Marshall's Grapes Brewery, Water Street, in 1885. Company registered in March 1888. Taken over by Greenall, Whitley & Co Ltd in 1958. Magee's Crown Brewery closed in October 1970, and the building was demolished in 1984.

The Albion Hotel on Moor Lane photographed in 1908, when the premises were being extended into the house on the corner of Hanover Street. The pub is advertising Leach's home brewed ales.

W T Settle

Rose & Crown Brewery, Cross Street

From the 1870s Robert Booth was the beerseller and brewer at the Rose & Crown beerhouse. William T Settle took over the business at the beginning of the twentieth century. Taken over by Dutton's Blackburn Brewery Ltd in 1951.

Joseph Sharman & Sons Ltd

Mere Hall Brewery

Founded in 1868 at the Crompton Brewery, Mill Street. The Mere Hall Brewery was built in 1874 and the private company was registered in 1896. John Hamer (Brewers) Ltd bought a controlling interest in 1926 and all the shares were acquired by George Shaw & Co Ltd of Leigh the following year. The brewery premises were sold by auction in 1928 for £3,100. The Sharman company was wound up in 1955.

Samuel Smith

Dog & Snipe Brewery, 181 Folds Road

The Dog & Snipe was a beerhouse and the brewery was in business by 1888. Samuel Smith owned several public houses in Bolton and Horwich. The brewery was closed by 1935.

Spa Wells Brewery Co Ltd

Park View Brewery, Spa Road

The company was registered in 1900 and sold to James Jackson & Sons Ltd in 1904. Under their direction the brewery became known as the Model Brewery. (See Howcroft's Brewery.)

William Tong & Sons Ltd

Diamond Brewery, Deane Road

In the 1850s William Tong kept a beerhouse on Pikes Lane (later Deane Road) and subsequently established the Diamond Brewery there, on the corner of Blackshaw Lane. A private company was registered in 1897. This was taken over by Walker Cain Ltd of Warrington in 1923, but continued as William Tong & Sons Ltd for many years afterwards with a head office in Mealhouse Lane.

Uncle Tom's Cabin Brewery

270-272 Lever Street

Henry Hilton was the licensee at the Uncle Tom's Cabin in the 1870s and by 1895 William Green was the brewer and beerseller. Mr Hilton's executors, Sarah Green and Emily Leach, inherited the business and in 1926 a limited company was registered. This was still brewing in the late 1930s.

Wingfield's Silverwell Brewery

15 Nelson Square

Thomas Wingfield, wine and spirit merchant, was established in Mawdsley Street in the 1820s. By the 1890s the firm had premises in Castle Street, Dorset Street and Nelson Square. A limited company was registered in October 1896 to take over T R Wingfield, brewers and wine and

The Prince Arthur Hotel, St John Street, in the 1920s. A few years earlier, brewers R Wood & Sons were based here

spirit merchants. The Manchester Brewery Company Ltd acquired the business in 1899, although Wingfields were still trading as wine and spirit merchants in the 1930s. Walker & Homfray Ltd of Salford took over the Manchester Brewery in 1912 and later merged with Wilsons Brewery of Newton Heath.

R Wood & Sons Ltd

Prince Arthur Brewery, St John Street
The Prince Arthur Hotel was a beerhouse and in the 1870s Robert Wood was a wholesale brewer there. A private company was registered in 1915, but this was short-lived and ceased trading after only a year or two.

J Hamer (Brewers) Ltd

Volunteer Brewery, Bromley Cross
Henry Hamer was running the Volunteer Inn during the 1860s; he was succeeded by John Hamer, who was listed as a publican and brewer by the 1890s. The limited company was registered in 1950 and the following year this was taken over by Dutton's Blackburn Brewery Co Ltd.

The Church Inn, Bamber Street, was a Tongs beerhouse at the beginning of the twentieth century, was later leased to Hydes of Manchester and was a Burtonwood house when it closed

Home brewed ales

Many of Bolton's licensed houses brewed their own beer in the nineteenth century and several of these are mentioned in Part Three. But by the early years of the twentieth century most of the home-brewing operations had closed as Magees, Sharmans, Tongs and others built up their substantial tied estates. Brewers' drays from the big companies became a familiar sight on the streets of Bolton, but some beerhouses continued to brew their own and Tillotson's Bolton Directory for 1932 shows the following beerhouses were among those still producing home-brewed ales:

British Oak, Derby Street
Colliers Arms, Chorley Old Road, Smithills
Golden Cup, Haigh Street
Greyhound Hotel, Manchester Road, Great Lever
Lord Raglan, Halliwell Road
Rope & Anchor, Kay Street
School Hill Hotel, School Hill

The Golden Cup on Haigh Street, still selling home brewed ales in the 1930s

Lancashire breweries

At the beginning of the twentieth century Lancashire boasted almost two hundred brewing companies, large and small. The following notes cover those mentioned in this book:

Boddingtons
Strangeways Brewery, Manchester. Still brewing, now owned by Whitbread.

Burtonwood
Still brewing.

Bury Brewery Company
The brewery was in George Street and was taken over by Thwaites in 1949, together with about eighty licensed houses.

Chadwicks Walmersley Brewery
The brewery on Walmersley Road can still be seen, although it was taken over by Walker & Homfrays of Salford in 1927, together with 43 licensed houses.

Cornbrook Brewery
Ellesmere Street, Chester Road, Manchester. The brewery and about 260 pubs were taken over by Charrington United Breweries in 1961. Brewing ceased about 1973.

Crown Brewing Company
Rochdale Road, Bury. Taken over by Duttons Blackburn Brewery in 1959 with 127 licensed houses.

Crowther's Star Brewery
Brook Street, Bury. Taken over by Wilsons Brewery in 1925.

Cunninghams Brewery
Owen Street, Warrington. In 1951 Cunninghams sold off sixty-five

licensed premises, thirty-four of them to Tetleys of Leeds. The company itself merged with Howcrofts of Bolton in 1969, but the business was wound up the same year.

Duttons Blackburn Brewery
Taken over by Whitbread in 1964 with about 800 licensed houses. Brewing continued as Whitbread West Pennines until 1978.

Empress Brewery
Parts of the brewery can still be seen on Chester Road, Old Trafford, Manchester. The company was taken over by Walkers of Warrington in 1929, together with 236 licensed houses.

Fairhurst Ltd
Warrington Lane, Wigan. The company owned about fifty licensed houses when it was wound up in 1921.

Grants Tower Brewery Company
Spring Bank Brewery, Ewood Bridge, near Edenfield. The company was taken over by John Kenyon Ltd of Barrowford in 1913.

Greenall Whitley
The Warrington brewery closed in 1991 and Greenalls are now a pub-owning company.

Groves & Whitnall
Regent Road Brewery. Taken over by Greenall Whitley in 1961, along with about 300 pubs and beerhouses. Brewing ceased in March 1972.

Holts
Derby Brewery, Empire Street, Cheetham, Manchester. Still brewing.

Hydes
Anvil Brewery, Moss Side, Manchester. Still brewing.

The Prince of Wales on Mount Street in 1961. It was a Wingfields house before being acquired by the Manchester Brewery Company and then by Wilsons

Lees
J W Lees & Co, Greengate Brewery, Middleton Junction. Still brewing.

Manchester Brewery Company
Britannia Brewery, Broadie Street, Ardwick. Taken over by Walker & Homfrays of Salford in 1912.

Openshaw Brewery Company
Victoria Brewery, West Gorton. Taken over by Hope & Anchor Breweries of Sheffield with 125 licensed houses in 1957.

The Spinners Arms, Mill Hill Street, in the 1920s. This was one of several Sharmans beerhouses acquired by Shaws of Leigh in 1927

Seeds
Richard Seed & Co Ltd, Spring Lane Brewery, Radcliffe. Taken over by Duttons Blackburn Brewery in 1938 with 56 licensed houses.

Shaws
George Shaw & Co Ltd, Brewery Lane, Leigh. Taken over by Walkers of Warrington in 1931 with 180 licensed houses, plus 58 under Sharmans.

Swales
J G Swales & Co Ltd, Junction Street, Hulme, Manchester. Taken over by Boddingtons in 1971 with 38 licensed houses.

Threlfalls
Cook Street Brewery, Salford. Merged with Chesters Brewery of Ardwick to form Threlfalls-Chesters in 1961. Taken over by Whitbread in 1967.

Thwaites
Blackburn. Still brewing.

Walkers of Warrington
Merged with Tetleys of Leeds in 1960.

Wilsons
Newton Heath Brewery, Manchester. Taken over by Watney Mann in 1960. Brewing at Newton Heath ceased in the 1980s.

Walker & Homfray
Woodside Brewery, Salford. Merged with Wilsons Brewery in 1949 with some 477 licensed houses.

Watson, Woodhead & Wagstaffe
Irwell Street, Salford. Merged with Walker & Homfrays in 1912 and wound up in 1923.

Whitefield Brewery Co
Higher Lane, Whitefield. The brewery was wound up in 1905.

Concerning Bolton evening closing times

In January 1865 Bolton Council received a petition from numerous ratepayers requesting the adoption of the Public House Closing Act, 1864, whereby public houses were to be compulsorily closed from 1.00am to 4.00am. The Council adopted the Act and accordingly local pubs had to close at 1.00am and not keep open, as many had done, for the whole of the 24 hours.

A new Licensing Act came into operation in August 1872 and was referred to in the Bolton Evening News as follows: 'Saturday was the first day on which the provisions of the Act were enforced. In the afternoon the police officers gave notice to the publicans and beersellers in the town that they would not be allowed to open their houses longer than - Sundays, Christmas Day and Good Friday, from 12.30 till 3.30 in the afternoon, and from six until ten o'clock in the evening; and on weekdays, from six in the morning until eleven at night'.

The first owner of the Pilkington Arms was a Mr Pilkington; it was later a tied house of the Park View Brewery and a Shaw's house when this photograph was taken in the 1920s

In more recent times, 1921 to be precise, a 10.00pm daily closing came into operation. Drinking hours were extended to 10.30pm Monday to Saturday inclusive in March 1959, and to 10.30pm on Sundays under the terms of the 1964 Licensing Act, which received Royal Assent in March 1964 and came into effect on January 1st 1965. In November 1961 the extra ten minutes 'drinking up time' was allowed. Hours were extended to 11.00pm on Fridays and Saturdays with effect from March 1962, and from April 1985 pubs were allowed to stay open until 11.00pm each weekday. 'All day' opening came into operation in 1989 and Sunday extended opening times in 1995.

The Standard Hotel, Gray Street. It once belonged to the Prince Arthur Brewery and was a Tongs house when this photograph was taken in the 1920s

Acknowledgements

I am grateful to Mr Leslie Gent, former Editor of the Bolton Evening News, for permission to reproduce many of the old photographs; Barry Mills and the staff of Bolton Reference Library for allowing me to peruse their photographic collection and for the use of directories and other records; Kevin Campbell, Bolton Borough Archivist, for the 1849 list of hostelries and for making available the Licensing Registers. Thanks also to the staff of the Borough Licensing Justices Department for earlier availability of the records and information from the 1999 Register. Details of the earliest Bolton alehouses are based on records in the Lancashire Record Office.

Thank you to Geoff Haslam for the photograph of the Commercial Hotel, Mr F Leech for the photograph of the former New Market Inn, Bridge Street; Chris Driver, formerly of the Bolton Museums Department, for the photographs of the Lower Nags Head. To John Hill for his help generally, Norman Johnson of Tetley-Walker, Malcolm Smith of Wilsons Brewery, Norman Kenyon, and Neil Richardson not only for his publishing expertise but also for allowing me to reproduce his photographs, for considerable research and helpful suggestions. Finally, thank you to colleagues and friends for information and useful advice, and anyone of the past and present who through writings or word of mouth has supplied essential details.